John White

THE GOLDEN COW

Materialism in the
Twentieth-Century Church

INTER-VARSITY PRESS
DOWNERS GROVE
ILLINOIS 60515

Third printing, December 1979

© *1979 by Inter-Varsity Christian
Fellowship of the United States of America*

*InterVarsity Press is the book-publishing
division of Inter-Varsity Christian Fellowship,
a student movement active on
campus at hundreds of universities,
colleges and schools of nursing. For information
about local and regional activities, write
IVCF, 233 Langdon St., Madison, WI 53703.*

*Distributed in Canada through InterVarsity Press,
1875 Leslie St., Unit 10,
Don Mills, Ontario M3B 2M5, Canada.*

*Bible quotations, unless otherwise stated,
are from the Revised Standard Version
of the Bible, copyrighted 1946,
1952,* © *1971, 1973 and are used by permission.*

*ISBN 0-87784-490-9
Library of Congress Catalog Card Number: 78-13884*

Printed in the United States of America

To my wife Lorrie
who stayed with me
on my pilgrimage
from disenchantment to
determination.

ACKNOWLEDGMENT

*It is customary to let the adversities
and ardors of editors go unsung.
The manuscript I originally wrote
raised one or two vexatious technical
problems, and I was so impressed
by the professional skill, the diplomacy and
the patience of Mr. Andrew
Le Peau and Dr. James Sire that
I do not hesitate to break with custom
and express my gratitude to them.*

1

THE PROPHET'S WHIP OF CORDS

He made the whip himself (Jn. 2:15). Therefore his act of enraged violence was premeditated, not an impulsive outburst. He made a plan and he carried it out. Seizing tables piled with coins he tossed them on their sides. An uproar of protesting and excited voices was heard amid crashes of heavy furniture on stone, tinkling of rolling coins, and the swish and crack of his whip. Sheep bleating, oxen lowing drowned out the muted sounds of the frightened pigeons.

Whether or not the whip bit deep into the flesh of human shoulders we do not know, though I suspect it lashed down on people as well as on animals. Some translations read that he turned over the stools of the pigeon sellers, and as likely as not he unseated some by doing so. They would lie sprawling as the panicked animals stumbled over them.

The miracle is that protests were as feeble as they were

vain. He would be sweating and panting with exertion, and there would be a calm purposefulness in his eyes that people could not face. Sheep, oxen, pigeons and people (who would snatch up whatever they had time to) were forced amid the hubbub through the gates.

Nor having done so much did he stop short. Each unsuspecting merchant arriving with more animals would be startled to find his way barred and a whip gripped in the menacing fist of the man with the unflinching gaze (Mk. 11:16).

It is false to assume that there was something supernatural about the awe he created. Though he was God, he called down no legion of angels to help him, nor is there any evidence that a mystical terror paralyzed the merchants. His control of the crowds was by a moral force, forged by his total lack of ambivalence and the money-changers' uneasy consciences. He was expressing what the common people deep within their hearts had known for years.

Like some modern clergy and academics who bleat inane polysyllables from pulpit and ivory tower, the religious authorities tried verbally to browbeat him. He dismissed them with a riddle. In their dismay they promptly began to plot his death (Mk. 11:17-18).

Again and again, both in the driving away of people and animals and in his teaching to the crowd the words recurred, "You shall not make my Father's house a house of trade" (Jn. 2:16). And waxing stronger, "Is it not written, 'My house shall be called a house of prayer for all the nations'? But you have made it a den of robbers" (Mk. 11:17). Few sermons are preached on the incident. We ourselves, as it were, stand among the crowd silent and disconcerted.

The Enraged Christ Commerce has flourished on the skirts of religion from time immemorial. The pencil bearing "Jesus Saves" in Christian bookstores is a modern example. But before I take issue with gospel pencils, let me ask, At what was the Son of God enraged?

It is an important question. In a life marked by gentleness and compassion this incident alone sees Jesus as a man of violence. Friends and foes alike were awed and bewildered. And since this is so we must assume that such a divergence must have unusual significance. The source of his rage must lie in a more flagrant evil than any other he encountered. His previous verbal outbursts against the Pharisees were hardly gentle. But only on this occasion did he resort to violence.

What was it about the traffic in coins and animals that offended him so deeply? "A house of prayer" he had called it, not a place of teaching nor yet a place of sacrifice. (He himself was to be the sacrifice.) What was in his mind?

It is interesting, as Cole points out (*The Gospel According to St. Mark*, pp. 177-79), that what enraged the priests and Pharisees was so different from what enraged the Son of God. Both they and he might be said to have had reverence for the Temple. But though priests and Pharisees were scandalized at the desecration caused by the noise of the children, they apparently saw nothing amiss with the commercialism in the courtyard. There is evidence that the High Priest may have owned some of the stores ransacked by Christ. Certainly the system flourished under the protection of the Temple hierarchy.

And why not? The moneychangers were performing a service for the worshipers. People journeyed to the Temple from many lands. Since Temple dues had to be paid in

Tyrian coinage, a convenient exchange developed for travelers with foreign currencies. Were the moneychangers not entitled to make a profit? How could they live if they performed the service gratis? What if a little cheating did take place occasionally? Was that not human nature? Can it ever be ruled out entirely?

Do we in the West share the outlook of the priests rather than that of Jesus? What do we say when small children run laughing and chasing inside our church buildings? Do we say, "Hush! This is God's house!" (If so we teach them a lie. God does not dwell in buildings of cement and steel, any more than in pseudo-Gothic showpieces. His people are his dwelling place.)

The priests' idea of reverence was perilously close to respect for themselves, for their religious system and all they in the pomp of their positions thought they stood for. They would have been shocked had you told them they no longer stood for Yahweh and his name. But you would have been telling the truth. They were guilty of idolatry. The dignity of the buildings was what mattered to them.

A place of prayer. In the purposes of God, the Temple was to be a place in which all nations might have access to him. Isaiah's prophecies must surely have been in the mind of Jesus as he cleansed the Temple. In their spiritual declension the Pharisees and Sadducees had lost true reverence for God. And though it hurts me deeply to say it, many churches in the West also seem to have no reverence for him either. Arrogantly, we worship our own institutions, our buildings, our programs. It is a sick and devilish worship for these things to reflect our glory, beaming our egocentric worship back upon ourselves to exalt us in the eyes of the world and of our religious competitors. We have become gods in our idolatrous religious empires.

The Prophet Christ   Jesus consumed with passion. Nowadays we have forgotten how to see him as prophet. He was God the Son, deity incarnate. He was man, sharing both our human estate and our human condition. He was our representative, our substitute, our sacrifice. He is now our compassionate High Priest. He is our Lord, our king, the captain of our salvation, our shepherd, our bread of life.

But prophet? Sure—*prophet,* priest and king, but.... We find it hard to think of him as prophet, so accustomed have we grown to seeing him in other terms. And as we view the details of his earthly ministry we unconsciously remove our "prophet" spectacles, seeing him as teacher, healer, fisher of men, the unrecognized Messiah, God the Son, the Son of man approaching Calvary with purposeful, unhurried steps. Perhaps we grow uneasy since to see him as prophet is to see him as some of his contemporaries saw him—*mere* prophet.

Yet he was the last great prophet, the greater-than-Moses prophet. He was the ultimate prophet who conferred gravely and in transcendent glory with his predecessors, Moses and Elijah, on the Mount of Transfiguration. He was the final member of the long prophetic line.

And whatever its unique characteristics, his ministry stood squarely in the prophetic tradition. He addressed the Word of the living God to the sinful, faithless leaders of God's people. The crudeness and violence of the old prophetic language became, in the prophet Jesus, violent action in the very center of religious life. Like the prophets who preceded him, he fearlessly defied established authority in the name of Yahweh.

To understand Jesus the prophet, we need to understand the prophetic tradition he stood in. He charged the Pharisees with idolatry in the same way the prophets of the Old Testament charged Israel with it. To bring their condemnation home, these ancient men of God accused the nation of prostitution. The people of Israel had sold themselves repeatedly to other gods even though their true spouse was God alone. The allurements of political security, social acceptability and economic advancement had wooed them often to beds of defilement.

Time has a way of mellowing the past, even of lending it charm and beauty. The stern denunciations of the prophets and the violent action of Jesus in the Temple stir us only in the way pictures in an art gallery do. We view them with wondering eyes, marveling that such dramatic power, such beauty can exist; yet as we pass into the hubbub of the streets, we leave the pictures behind. But if the prophets would step out of the pictures or Jesus were to leap, whip in hand, from the pages of the Gospels to confront us, how would we respond?

It is just such a possibility I would like us to take seriously in this book. There is an uncanny similarity between our day and that of ancient Israel. God's ancient people worshiped the Baalim: we worship a materialistic golden cow. At heart many of us have a greed for things. We have made the world's agenda of status seeking our own. Unquestioningly we have adopted the world's techniques of gaining influence and security. And it has worked. We are flushed with success. We have made *Time* and *Newsweek*. Yet can we be sure that we are featured in national magazines for the best of reasons? Is it because of our godliness and our love for our neighbors, or is it because we have grown large enough to have political influence? Have we attracted society's attention by reflecting the beauty of our Lord, or have we prostituted ourselves, being successfully peddled to the public by public relations experts?

This book is about materialism in the church. Another Temple cleansing is needed. The church today is a prostitute and needs to be brought back. Our worship of the cow must end. In the next two chapters I define my terms. What is a prostitute? How did the prophets use the concept of prostitution? Chapter four considers Christ's teaching on the place of possessions. Chapter five looks at the way in which the church today has followed mammon rather than her bridegroom, Christ. Chapters six through eight discuss the ways our local churches, our parachurch organizations and our Christian businesses have done this. Chapter nine considers how materialistic attitudes affect not only the way we handle money and property but the way we approach our fellow human beings in evangelism. (Do we treat them as things we win or as people together with whom we kneel before the throne of God?)

I close in chapter ten by considering the future of the church of Christ. Persecution from the powers of darkness is sure to come. Divine judgment on those who are unfaithful is equally certain. God takes no sadistic pleasure in it. Rather he is a God who weeps over our sins, who grieves over our waywardness. He yearns for us to realize that there is no place for two treasures in our hearts. He seeks to win back his bride who has found another lover. It is time to recognize what we have done and to repent of the sins into which we have fallen.

2

THE PROPHETS' WHIP OF WORDS

Accusing God's people of harlotry was a startling way to call attention to their sins. But this is exactly what the prophets did. When we look at the passages where they do so, we become aware that more than name calling is involved. Ezekiel, for instance, accused Jerusalem of being a prostitute. But did you ever hear of a prostitute who paid her clients to do business with her? That's what Ezekiel accused Jerusalem of doing (Ezek. 16:31-34).

I ask the question for two reasons. First, it reminds us that when the prophets called Jerusalem a whore, they may not have been using the word as we might ourselves. We know what a whore is. When we call a woman (or a man for that matter) a whore, we feel we know what we are talking about. But second, the issue at hand is not what *we* think when we use such distasteful words but what God thinks.

If we were to turn for a definition of harlotry to sociology, or even if we were to lug from our bookshelves our largest and heaviest dictionaries and encyclopedias, we could have a good, perhaps even a salacious, discussion. But much of what we might say would be beside the point. I take my hat off to the learning of sociologists and lexicographers, but when we look at something from God's perspective their learning may not help, for they do not concern themselves with the prophets.

Many hundreds of years have passed since these men and women of God thundered their denunciations against Israel's and Judah's whoredoms. When the prophets raised their voices they did so because God was displeased with his people. To be sure, he was displeased in particular ways and about particular things. Hence the inspired and metaphorical use of the term *whore*. The real issue, however, is not the technical appropriateness of comparing call girls and religious institutions, but whether God is displeased with his people—displeased, that is to say, in the same ways he was when the prophets charged Israel and Judah with whoredom.

Our starting point then must be with the prophets. Why did they speak thus? What had so enraged God? What did he have in mind in comparing his people with those involved in sexual immorality?

Let me return to Ezekiel's whore. Her absurd discount rate raises a question. To take a loss on your business means you must be pretty desperate to stick with it. (At once we see not only the pathos of Israel's plight but that we are dealing with matters of the heart.) Jerusalem may not exactly have loved her lovers. Prostitutes seldom do. But when they do, they become desperate indeed. Ezekiel is assessing a wretchedness which implies an inner spiritual sickness. While he alludes to certain sinful practices in Israel, he is more concerned with the condition of the heart that gives rise to them than with the practices themselves.

Isaiah, Jeremiah, Ezekiel and Hosea all have something to tell us about the whoredoms of God's people. Isaiah and Jeremiah have the least to say, Hosea the most. Hosea's own relationship with his promiscuous wife gave him, in fact, at the cost of great personal pain, the profoundest insight into God's attitude to his people. Ezekiel utters a beautiful allegory about the foundling whom God made his bride, but who betrayed her divine husband. But when we look to the prophets for a definition of a whore, a definition that is, in terms of what constitutes spiritual whoredom, they seem to give us unexpected answers.

If we look carefully at the context in which such words as *whore, whoredom* and others are found, we shall gain a substantial part of the answer. Scholars may rightly add certian footnotes to what we decide, but the main thrust of what the prophets are saying seems clear enough.

Sons, Asses, Oxen, Harlots: Isaiah When, for instance, Isaiah talks about Jerusalem's whoredom (Is. 1:21-23), his specific charges concern the adulteration of precious metals and the watering down of alcoholic beverages. He goes on to accuse Jerusalemites of bribery, corruption and murder. The men and women of his day, then, were guilty of commercial dishonesty (exploitation of the consumer), legal corruption and violent oppression.

As we look at the wider context of the verses, however, we see that God uses other metaphors to express his grief over his people's sins. They are sons rebelling against their fa-

17

ther (Is. 1:2). They are worse than oxen who at least know their owner and donkeys who at least respond to their master (Is. 1:3). Rebellious sons, stubborn asses, forgetful oxen and an unrighteous harlot, all four images are used to describe how God sees a people who have forsaken social justice

The images used have one point in common: God's people, in sinning as they do have forgotten *who they are and to whom they belong.* The ox and the ass behave as though they were their own masters. The son denies his filial duty.

We might ask why the prophet does not simply state this. Why does he not put it in plain language? "God is shocked at your corruption, your violence, your exploitation. In behaving as you have you have forgotten who you are and to whom you belong." What could be more effective in awakening the people than bold, plain speaking?

I would suggest he uses the image of harlotry for two related reasons: Israel's relationship with God could aptly be compared with a sexual relationship, and the word *harlot* had in itself a shock value.

What feeble things words are! Or, to put it more accurately, how clever the human heart is in resisting them! The problem with Jerusalem's populace is the same as that of many Christians today. They were busily religious. They crowded the Temple courts with their sacrifices, oblivious to their inconsistencies, serenely unaware of Yahweh's grief and rage (Is. 1:12-15). God therefore selects the most stinging word that could be chosen to shake his people from their complacency: "How the faithful city has become a harlot" (Is. 1:21). *Asses* and *oxen,* yes. *Sons,* that word too is altogether acceptable. But *harlot!* The word is offensive, shocking.

Let me pause a moment to draw a conclusion, a conclusion we can test as we look at the rest of the prophets. The Holy Spirit's inspiration of a term like *harlot, whore* or *prostitute* is designed to sting people into shocked awareness that their sins (whatever those sins might be) enrage God because his people have forgotten *who they are and to whom they rightly belong.*

If what I say is true, then you see what a waste of time it would be to fuss over a precise definition of the word *harlot.* To us, what makes a prostitute is sex for cash. We distinguish prostitutes from other sexual sinners in that whereas some people "do it for love," prostitutes "do it for money." We even use the infinitive *to prostitute* metaphorically. Artists talk about prostituting their art when they descend to produce inferior works to please the populace or purely to make money. We must be careful, if I am right, not to fall into the trap of imposing our own ideas of prostitution on the prophet's use of the words. Isaiah used the term *harlot* to sting people into realizing they had betrayed their identity and their loyalty. Let us look at the other prophets to see whether they, too, use the term in the same way.

Crude but Effective: Jeremiah   Jeremiah is crude and graphic as he speaks of Jerusalem's harlotry. Repeating Yahweh's own words he writes, "I myself will lift up your skirts over your face, and your shame will be seen. I have seen your abominations, your adulteries and neighings, your lewd harlotries, on the hills in the field" (Jer. 13:26-27). Horror and contempt are obvious. Jeremiah seems to be finding the most scathing expression available to goad Jerusalem.

But what sins does he label harlotry? Throughout the

book he refers to different failures. In the immediate context Jeremiah seems to refer to the fact that Judah has gone a-whoring after other gods. Idolatry is the sin he has in mind.

Moreover if you look carefully at the verses I quoted above, you will notice not one but several expressions all referring to the same sins: "... your abominations, your adulteries and neighings, your lewd harlotries...." He piles one phrase on another in an attempt to emphasize how wretched, how shameful Judah's behavior had been. Word studies are hardly necessary. To play with the etymology of the passage would be to do what C. S. Lewis describes as trying to see fern seed while remaining blind to an elephant standing ten yards away. What comes through overwhelmingly is God's reprehension for what his people are doing.

It would seem possible then to apply the same principle we discovered in Isaiah. God's people have forgotten *who they are and to whom they belong*. The chosen people, the privileged possessors of the Law and of the mercy seat are fooling with petty little demons. They are violating their covenant relationship with God, oblivious to their heinous offense of forgetting the Most High.

Bribing Your Lovers: Ezekiel Ezekiel's treatment of the theme is lengthy, moving and full of allusions to Jerusalem's history. In Ezekiel 16 she is portrayed as an infant abandoned at birth, rescued, brought to full womanhood, espoused, cleansed and clothed as a princess by the Most High. God had no reason to pity so despicable and unattractive an infant, yet he treated her with royal grace and kindness.

She had become a harlot by worshiping idols and by making military alliances with Egypt, Assyria and Chaldea. She had forsaken the true God for false gods and had placed her trust in powerful neighbors rather than in the arm of the Lord. Vividly Ezekiel describes the shameful exposure and humiliation that await her but hints at the end of the chapter of an ultimate redemption and restoration.

Just as the other prophets did, Ezekiel uses the term *harlot* or *whore* as a lash not as a precisely defined word. It appears many times in the chapter before he eventually clarifies it. "You were not like a harlot, because you scorned hire," Ezekiel says to Jerusalem. "Adulterous wife, who receives strangers instead of her husband! Men give gifts to all harlots; but you gave your gifts to all your lovers, bribing them to come to you from every side for your harlotries. So you were different from other women in your harlotries: none solicited you to play the harlot; and you gave hire, while no hire was given to you; therefore you were different. Wherefore, O harlot, hear the word of the Lord..." (Ezek. 16:31-35).

Two things are clear. First, the word *harlot* in Ezekiel's day meant what *prostitute* means today. He spells out the details explicitly. At the same time he makes it clear that he is not concerned with the precise commercial negotiations by which people of his day (as well as of our own) might define harlotry, but with the horror of the betrayal of a sacred relationship.

But notice, second, the difference between God's perspective and our own. If we were to set men or women upon a scale of sexual virtue, most of us would place a prostitute lower on the ladder than an adulterer or adulteress. All are sinners, but prostitution seems to belong on a lower rung. Adultery is bad enough, but in the back of our minds an excuse suggests itself. At least the adulterers may have cared for each other. It was not a cold commercial contract where a body was sold for sex.

If we read again the passage from Ezekiel, however, we see that it overturns our standards. It is as though Ezekiel is saying, "A harlot at least works for pay. But you are worse than a harlot. You actually pay lovers to come to you." To us the greater evil is the commercialization of sex. To God it is the treachery, the ingratitude, the violation of a holy relationship, and its chief shame is the need to solicit and to purchase from inferior sources what a holy God had always given freely.

And when we remember that the one who so offends God was once a filthy baby lying abandoned in the desert, how much greater the offense becomes! Harlotry grieved God because when Jerusalem committed it she forgot who she was, *from whence she came* and to whom she belonged. It follows that whenever we forget the same things, we are on the brink of spiritual harlotry.

Ezekiel makes it clear that God is a God of passion. Jerusalem's treachery did not leave him unmoved or indifferent. "So will I satisfy my fury on you, and my jealousy shall depart from you; I will be calm, and no more be angry. Because you have not remembered the days of your youth, but have enraged me . . ." (Ezek. 16:42-43). It is left to Hosea, however, to give us some sense of the range of God's feelings toward a treacherous spouse.

In Love with a Harlot: Hosea Hosea married a harlot, Gomer. Whether or not she was a harlot by trade before

Hosea married her is not altogether clear. But clearly there was a serious question about the paternity of their first three children. Gomer eventually left home and wound up for sale in the slave market where Hosea purchased her, took her back home, treated her with restraint, firmness and kindness. He tells us little of the turbulence of his own feelings, but his subsequent prophecies show that his experience with Gomer opened his heart to an understanding of God's attitude to Israel, the harlot whom God sought to woo back to himself.

The Holy Spirit often makes us aware of God's own attitudes and feelings by causing us to pass through deep waters. I well remember an army officer who years ago attended the Keswick Convention in Britain, an annual event encouraging Christian commitment. With a bet of ten pounds he claimed he "could go right through Keswick unscathed, untouched." Beneath his bravado was an aching emptiness. One night after conversing with him I found myself weeping bitterly in the fields, overwhelmed by sorrow at his helpless plight. He seemed to be a cork, passively tossed about on crosscurrents of ideas, with no ability to control the direction he was moving in.

I do not often weep for others, nor am I inclined to react emotionally to conventions, yet there seemed no bottom to my sorrow. Suddenly in the darkness I had a strange sense of the Lord's presence. It seemed as though he was saying to me, "I see your little pool of sorrow. Why do you not let it flow into my great ocean?" It was then that for the first time I *saw* and *felt* something of the immense compassion of the Savior, so much so that my grief was turned into worship. I am glad my friend's restoration was delayed long enough for me to make my own discovery.

We can only imagine some of Hosea's intense grappling with bewilderment, despair, rage, revulsion, jealousy, love, pain, tenderness. Had God actually commanded him to marry Gomer? Could God be the source of such pain and tragedy? What did God want him to do now that she had abandoned him? " 'Go again, love a woman who is beloved of a paramour and is an adulteress; even as the LORD loves the people of Israel, though they turn to other gods and love cakes of raisins.' So I bought her for fifteen shekels of silver and a homer and a lethech of barley" (Hos. 3:1-2).

If Ezekiel was made aware of the terrors of divine judgments against Jerusalem's harlotry, Hosea became aware of more. To him was given a vision of God's unending tenderness to the bride of his choice through experiences he himself underwent. From his own pains and joys he could bear witness to God's mercy by prophetic utterances of unusual insight. More than this he was himself a flesh-and-blood example to Israel of enduring faithfulness in the face of perfidy. He became, if I may use the expression loosely but reverently, the faithfulness of God made incarnate in the eyes of his fellow Israelites.

Hosea gives the fullest and most complete picture of God's attitude in the face of harlotry. Once again we find terms like *harlot* and *adulteress* used synonymously and interchangeably. Harlotry is in fact defined as "forsaking the LORD" (Hos. 1:2). A careful reading of the book will confirm the basic principle I've already repeated: we commit harlotry by violating *who we are, from whence we came and to whom we belong.* It matters less *how* we violate these things than the fact that we dishonor God by doing so.

Hosea also makes us aware of the passions and reactions of a holy God, just as Ezekiel does. Ezekiel spoke of rage.

Hosea speaks of compassion and tenderness. "Therefore, behold, I will allure her, ... and speak tenderly to her. ... and make the Valley of Achor a door of hope. ... And I will betroth you to me for ever; I will betroth you to me in righteousness and in justice, in steadfast love, and in mercy" (Hos. 2:14-15, 19).

God is indeed a God of passion. But how are we to understand his feelings? Words like *jealousy, rage* or *tenderness* convey images to our minds based on our human experiences. This in itself may not constitute too serious a difficulty for we are made in the image of God. Nevertheless there are dangers in assuming our emotions are identical with his.

How could they be? We are fallen: he is holy. We are finite: he is infinite. We are in time and subject to change: God inhabits eternity and is immutable.

I will leave to those more competent than I the questions that such considerations raise. Obviously they are immense, and perhaps no one here on earth can resolve them completely. But of two things we may be sure. First, in considering the feelings of God we are treading on holy ground. We must remove our sandals and walk softly with heads bowed low, ready to fall on our faces if need be. Second, while we may not fully understand what it means to say God feels, the Holy Spirit himself reveals to us that he *does*.

His feelings exist in relation to us. His jealous rage and tenderness burn against Christians guilty of idolatry, guilty of holding material things in higher regard than God. We do well to tremble lest we forget who we are, from whence we came and to whom we belong. For our God is a God of fire.

3

THE PROPHETS AND THE SHAME OF NAKEDNESS

The God of the prophets seems harsh and sadistic when he threatens his harlot bride. "I myself will lift up your skirts over your face, and your shame will be seen" (Jer. 13:26). "I will gather all your lovers . . . against you from every side, and will uncover your nakedness to them, that they may see all your nakedness" (Ezek. 16:37). "I will take away my wool and my flax, which were to cover her nakedness. Now I will uncover her lewdness in the sight of her lovers, and no one shall rescue her out of my hand" (Hos. 2:9-10).

Where do the prophets gain the notion of so crude and indecent a form of punishment? Does it reflect the culture they were part of? Were harlots so treated in Judah and Israel in their day? Would a betrayed husband normally act toward an erring spouse in this way?

The answer to these questions is no.

Certainly terrible penalties might fall on a harlot's head. A priest's daughter who prostituted herself might be burned to death (Lev. 21:9). Other prostitutes might be stoned (Deut. 22:21; Jn. 8:5). Shameful public exposure however is mentioned only by the prophets, and even then, only in relation to God's people. To my knowledge there is no evidence that harlots were ever so treated. It is possible that a harlot sold in a slave market might have been exposed to display her desirable attributes to lascivious buyers. But this would not be punishment. It would be social abuse.

Let me put the matter another way. Let us suppose that Jeremiah, Ezekiel and Hosea wrote as they did because of what they had seen. In that case why do they never mention in their prophecies burning or stoning, the customary fates of harlots under the law? We must conclude that the exposure so consistently threatened by the prophets has little if anything to do with how harlots of their time were punished. Each prophet in his turn, inspired by the same Spirit, wrote of God's dealings with spiritual unfaithfulness. Stoning might be appropriate for the physical sin, but public exposure was to be the fate of the spiritual harlot.

The language is crude and graphic. Had only one of the three alluded to the matter we might have dismissed it as unimportant. Yet as we read what each has written we almost get the feeling that they had met and reached a common agreement, so closely do their words and ideas coincide. Yet we know that no such collusion ever took place. The shocking notion of a harlot being stripped, mocked and exposed to the contempt of her lovers is inspired by the Spirit of God. It refers to the fate of his people.

We must therefore ask why so crude a measure was to be adopted. Was God being malicious? Or was there some strange blend of justice and healing in his terrible and shameful sentence?

Naked and Ashamed We humans are ashamed when we are naked. (There are exceptions to the rule, exceptions which if we examine them closely reinforce it.) To be naked is to be ashamed. In nightmares we find ourselves on the street or at work or in church partly or completely unclothed, struggling to conceal ourselves in any available crevice. Our nightmares reflect our underlying terror of exposure.

The shame seems to be confined to human beings. Animals and birds may be ashamed if we disfigure their coats or their plumage. But in so doing we are not denuding them, but interfering with the form of their bodies. The shame they feel may be related to our shame of nakedness but is not the same. Some dogs will slink by with their tails between their legs if certain parts of their anatomy are trimmed. But this is no different from the reaction of a naval friend of mine who became unpopular on our ship. His colleagues shaved off one half of his beard and the other half of his mustache. His hairy face had been his pride and joy. Its gross disfigurement was a source of humiliation and shame.

And to be sure the element of being different from what we are accustomed to, different from the way we like to see ourselves is part of the shame we feel at being naked. But it is only a part, and by no means the most important part.

The specific human shame of nakedness has to do with sexuality. Divorce sexuality from nakedness and its shame diminishes greatly or may disappear altogether. People who live in nudist colonies (for whom I offer neither de-

fense nor apology) know this. People who do not live in
nudist colonies fail to comprehend it because in their minds
sex and nakedness cannot be altogether divorced. A simple
example of the separation of sex from nakedness would be
that of getting undressed for a medical examination. For
some people it is embarrassing, for others not. But the fact
that the situation has (or should have) no sexual overtones
reduces the shame of the exposure.

Our shame of nakedness is likewise a part of our fallen
condition. The original pair knew they were naked after
they had sinned. They hid. After their pathetic attempts
to cover their bodies, the Lord himself mercifully clothed
them. The shame of nakedness and the need for clothing
were born on that day.

Whether or not their shame had sexual overtones is not
clear. The sacred narrative makes no allusions to sexual
relations before the Fall, but mentions them explicitly after
it. Sin did not *produce* sexuality, but sin clearly made a
change in its expression.

Of course there are people nowadays who display their
bodies publicly on beaches, in movies, at nightclubs or in
sexual orgies. In most cases the exposure is sex related. It
defies shame, sometimes for the sexual titillation of observers and for the financial profit of the exhibitionist. It
is sham*eless.*

But shamelessness in such cases is extreme sickness. It is
sin carried (in a sexual area) to its utmost limit. A certain
degree of shame about one's nakedness is healthy. To lose
one's shame is to become less human. God did not respond
to Adam and Eve's shame by telling them not to be silly, but
by covering their shame. We are to be clothed.

Anthropologists might point out that some savage tribes

live naked. I do not know all naked savage tribes but I know some. I also know that nakedness to us is not always nakedness to them. A string, an ornament, an armband, a decoration—symbolic perhaps, but terribly important to the wearer—signify clothing.

We may assume then that our shame of nakedness, an attribute of our fallen condition, is essentially sex related. As we read the prophets this must be doubly obvious. In exposing the bodies of harlots God is doing something explicitly sexual. He is exposing her lewdness, her abominations, her harlotries. It is this, in fact, that makes the retribution so harsh, so terrible.

Exposed and Known We humans are strange. In addition to the need to remain clothed and covered we have an equally deep need to expose ourselves. The exposure can be precious, enrapturing and holy within the bonds of lifelong marital commitment. It is not primarily a sensual experience though sensuality plays a part. Rather it represents the hunger we feel to be known and accepted as we really are for our naked, secret selves. A hunger likewise to know, to reach out to another being and end the isolation and the aloneness for which neither of us was ever designed. ("It is not good that the man should be alone.")

Life under God is not to be lived in isolation but in relationship with another. To be isolated is not to be fully human. But the drive to expose and to be exposed has dangers. In its proper place it is a gateway by which we dimly perceive God's relationship with his people. Misplaced, misused it becomes a scourge—destructive, deadening and alienating. Its delights can turn poisonous. Its end can be cold disgust.

Physical strength was given to us to build, to protect, to guard and uplift the young and the weak. Yet the same strength can be a cruelly brutal scourge, murdering and pillaging the defenseless. In the same way our sex-linked drive to expose and to be exposed can be either a blessing or a curse to us. It has to do with a most sensitive area at the core of our beings. Its potential for the deepest human satisfaction gives it an equal potential for bitterness and pain. It can lead to human fulfillment but with equal ease to emptiness and cold despair.

So we are driven to expose as well as to clothe ourselves. I must not, of course, leave you with the impression that sexual relations make a marriage. A marriage based solely on eroticism is doomed to fail. We live in an age of genital athletics, of ecstatic achievements. They have to do with techniques. Technique at best is but a poor means to a great end and at worst a poor means to a worthless end—sensual delight for its own sake. It is not to such things I refer. Rather I speak of the *purpose* of exposure, that of knowing and being known. With good reason the first account of sexual relations in the Bible was translated at one time, "And Adam *knew* his wife." For the purpose of sexual exposure is to accept and to be accepted: to accept another as he or she is and to be accepted as I truly am, to love and to be loved, to be faithful and to know fidelity, to be bound in a physical and emotional bond to which two persons commit themselves till death do them part.

Yet even the most satisfying marital relationship can never meet our deepest needs. There is something within us that cries for more—not for more sex or even for more closeness in human relationships but for that which human closeness awakens in us, the hunger that makes us human and different from animals. "For thou has made us for thyself," wrote Augustine, a millennium and a half ago, "and our hearts are restless till they find their rest in thee."

When Adam hid, he hid from God. Yet he and his descendants have ever since, whether consciously or not, yearned to dare to expose themselves to God again: yearned, yet feared exposure to the Most High; yearned for the closeness for which they were created.

Israel knew a little (not much, but a little) of that closeness. God had revealed (exposed) himself to this people and they, in fear and trembling, to him. But the covenant had been violated, the intimacy outrageously betrayed. The hunger in his people remained. In their folly they looked elsewhere to satisfy it, ignorant of the blasphemous obscenity they committed. They played the harlot.

We may take it that as a general rule the more sacred the trust, the more terrible is its betrayal. We are shocked, for instance, to learn of a mother who murders her baby. Cynical as we may be, it troubles us when a president betrays his country for personal ends. To let someone down about a minor matter, say, to forget a dental appointment, is trivial. To break a promise to help someone in need seems more serious. If, for example, I solemnly swore to you to take care of your children in the event of your death, it would be treachery for me to abandon them to their fate and to ignore my solemn commitment. For this reason the betrayal of the trust within which it became possible for a man and a woman to disclose themselves to each other becomes a terrible matter.

It would seem to follow logically that the public exposure of such a sin should be correspondingly shameful. Yet so cynical is the age we live in, so jaded our appetites for the sensational and the horrific, that the mere disclosure of the facts of betrayals has begun to pall. We eat the news of a movie star's latest switch of partners with our daily bread. We drink presidential corruptions with our coffee. And though exposure by the media may be embarrassingly painful to the person exposed, it hardly affects the rest of us. Even the pastor's affair with his secretary fails to bring us to our knees. We swallow it with relish.

Yet however cynical we may become, there is something about physical exposure that reaches all of us. I do not suggest it as an appropriate course of action, but if the erring pastor and his lover were displayed *unclothed* before us, we would no longer react with relish but with profound shame.

A friend of mine who spent his childhood in Alexandria, Egypt, describes a quarrel between a young Arab boy and his mother. Children and adults alike began to turn and listen as the two voices were raised in anger. The boy's fluency in vituperation, profanity and obscenity gave him an advantage. Suddenly the woman in exasperation raised her skirts and exposed herself to the boy as well as to the crowd.

"Look!" she cried. "This is where you came from, and don't you ever forget it!"

A silence which could be felt fell on everybody in the street and most of all on the shame-stricken boy.

God's Honor, Israel's Shame   Judah and Israel were to experience this same quality of shame. Not only they, but the onlookers, the nations around with whom they had "committed adultery" were to be shocked into an awareness of God's standards and God's concern. The exposure was to have exactly the kind of effect on surrounding nations as the Alexandrian woman's action on the crowds. For God's own honor was at stake. Israel's shame was not only a punishment for her but a testimony to the world, a witness to the standards of a holy God.

We in the modern church confuse witness with reputation. We conceal facts discreetly, saying, "It wouldn't be a very good testimony if this sort of thing got around." Discretion is valuable in its place. What we sometimes forget is that the world around us is well aware of what goes on in our congregations and institutions. Truth will out. And as people begin to realize not only that our standards of behavior are no different from theirs but that we tolerate and conceal what we profess to abhor, our preaching becomes an empty parroting in their ears. It is not sin which destroys our witness, but *concealed* and *tolerated* sin. If we were to deal with sin more openly, more radically, and to be less concerned with our reputations, our witness would in fact be powerful.

And among our chief sins, as I have already indicated, is that of our materialism. It has invaded us as a cancer eats out the inner vitals of a living body. It must be dealt with by radical surgery. Therefore we must look at some aspects of it in later chapters so that we may recognize it when we see it. If we do not expose it to be cured, then to be sure God will.

If we fail to deal with sin, God himself may have to deal with it publicly so the world may know that he exists and that his standards remain unchanged. He may shock the world and shame us by revealing our nakedness for all to see. We shall cry in sickened dismay as we vainly try to cover our blushing faces or to turn our heads to one side.

35

4

TREASURE AND HEART

We live in a materialistic world divided by iron and bamboo curtains into two materialistic camps, those of capitalist materialism and of communist materialism. To Christians in the West the communist variety seems infinitely more sinister. Under Western materialism the church flourishes and religious groups are not only free but enjoy tax concessions. Many churches are full. Superbly prepared literature grows in volume and sales. A missionary movement on an unprecedented scale has carried the Christian gospel to all parts of the earth.

Yet volume is no substitute for quality. In the other half of the world where Christians are much less affected by the temptation of our kind of materialism, we find evidence of a spirit and a joy (in spite of suffering) which makes Western Christianity seem hollow.

Christians in China, in Russia, in Eastern Europe, in Africa, in Cuba live lives of incredible heroism and go on bearing witness with gladness. Beaten, imprisoned, vilified and fiendishly tortured, their joy rises unquenchable and their faith stands unshakable. We make a mistake when we glibly assert that what the Western church needs is persecution. We must be grateful for our freedom. The real explanation of the difference between the underground churches of the East and the showpiece churches of the West has to do with materialism.

Communist materialism is doctrinaire and oppressive. Capitalist materialism is pragmatic and cancerous. Communist materialism claims that matter is all there is. Western materialism assumes that matter is all that *matters*. Many people who would never consider themselves to be materialists in the strict sense of the term, nevertheless live as though material things were of supreme importance. My definitions are rough and ready, and my general statements are oversimplifications. Nevertheless they will serve my present purposes, for I am not writing a sociological treatise.

My definition of Western materialism might appear to exclude Christians. No Christian would agree (that is, if the matter were put to him or her as an abstract proposition) that matter is all that matters for our very faith negates the assertion. Yet if our behavior (as distinct from our verbal profession) is examined, many of us who call ourselves Christians begin to look more like materialists. We talk of heaven but we strive for things.

Yet Christians are rarely happy as materialists. Heaven tugs at us too vigorously. We find ourselves apologizing for our new cars or our larger houses. This tug of war renders most Christians ill at ease and at times ineffective.

Occasionally you may come across Christians who pursue wealth successfully yet who show no evidence of this struggle. I would say either that their financial success is coincidental, that is to say they find it immaterial whether they make another million dollars or not (for there are some millionaires who do not care a fig for money) or else that their Christian profession is false. In the latter case they experience no heavenly tug in their hearts.

The misery of a Christian torn between heaven and material things can be pitiful. A self-made Cantonese importer invited my wife and me to dinner once. His house was breathtaking—a fortress outside and all softness and luxury within. In the foyer stood an artificial tree, perhaps five feet high, whose leaves and flowers were exquisitely fashioned from clusters of semiprecious stones. Ornate cabinets displayed valuable treasures. His tableware looked like solid gold but we did not dare to ask.

Our host was about sixty years old and displayed a considerable knowledge of Scripture, yet as he talked there was no glow of joy about him. He told us he planned to make enough money to spend his closing years in serving the Lord "without being a burden on anybody." (The tableware alone would have kept some of us going in Christian work for quite a while.)

He never did get to serve the Lord. He had sold his heritage for stone and metal trinkets inside a painted fortress. He would have agreed that spiritual things matter more than material security, but his behavior contradicted his professed beliefs. Riches had coiled like a living vine around his heart, slowly strangling his love for God and people.

Christians disagree about what the New Testament teaches on riches and possessions. Down the centuries there have been disproportionately wealthy Christians and others embracing voluntary poverty, giving away their possessions to serve God and their fellow human beings. What does Christ teach?

The Social Milieu If we are to interpret accurately Jesus' teaching about material wealth, we must have some idea of the social context in which his words were uttered. Dick France discusses the matter in *Third Way* magazine ("Serving God or Mammon," May 18, 1978). "The socio-economic situation of the time of Jesus is vividly illustrated by several of his parables. They reveal a sharply class-structured society, with landowners, stewards, tenant-farmers, day laborers and slaves. It was a situation in which the few could dress in purple and fine linen and feast sumptuously every day, while beggars sat at the gates; where capital steadily accumulated in the hands of the rich, while the ordinary free man lived under the threat of slavery for debt."

France quotes an estimate that because of the double burden of religious dues and Roman taxes, a total taxation of about forty per cent would be exacted from an average income, *not* including unjust exactions of local tax collectors (F. C. Grant, *The Economic Background to the Gospels*, p. 26).

Two things interest France: the social background of Jesus and his followers, and the chosen lifestyle they adopted. The social background appears to have been middle class. Joseph, the earthly father of Jesus, ran a carpentry business and might even have employed workers. Matthew was a tax collector. Peter, James and John had shares in a boat and in fishing equipment for their fishing enterprise. They too may have employed extra hands. Other followers included the wife of Herod's steward and women who "provided for them out of their means." Joseph was far from wealthy (the öffering of two turtle doves rather than a lamb at Jesus' presentation at the Temple indicates this) but he was a long way from being at the bottom of the economic ladder.

The lifestyle Jesus adopted, and which he encouraged his disciples to adopt, involved a renunciation (or at least a forsaking) of any private property other than the clothes they all wore daily, and a dependence on God to supply their needs through the generosity of the people to whom they ministered. They received food and lodging on their journeys, may have been more especially indebted to people such as Lazarus, Martha and Mary, and probably received gifts of money from time to time (though there is no record of their ever soliciting funds).

What they possessed they seemed to share in common, Judas taking care of the distribution. From their meager resources they probably still gave to the poor. (The protest against the waste of the ointment poured on the Lord's feet implies that giving to the poor was their practice—Jn. 12:4-5.)

Their chosen lifestyle raises a number of questions. Was it intended to be a model for all followers of Jesus? Was it perhaps a model for "full-time workers"? Are there two classes of followers of Jesus, those who forsake all and live a hand-to-mouth existence as they serve him, and those who supply such workers from their capital and income?

There can be no question that during the New Testament period no universal economic practice was adopted by Christians. Many early Christians sold their goods and shared with others in the church at Jerusalem. It does not seem to have been expected that the practice should be universal.

Many scholars suggest that the generous sharing in Jerusalem was occasioned by the hardship of those converts who had come from a great distance for the feast and who had stayed on. Others point to the probable poverty of even local converts. The action of the Jerusalem church is often criticized by modern Christians who feel that the subsequent appeals to other churches would not have been necessary had the rash generosity of the wealthier Christians been more temperate. It would have been better, they feel, to have been less generous and to have encouraged more industry.

Yet is it not possible that we fear having to share our own resources with Christians in need? Where in the modern world do we find the kind of love and generosity which makes church members sell homes and cars that the hardships of other Christians might be met? Are there no local economic hardships among God's people? If there is no suggestion that the Jerusalem pattern should become universal, neither do the Epistles utter a breath of criticism of the Jerusalem church. When funds were being raised across Asia Minor and Europe to continue to help the Jerusalem poor, it seems to have occurred to no one to blame the situation on economic mismanagement.

There is no doubt, however, that both among the early followers of Jesus and in the epoch of the New Testament church there existed two economic patterns. To quote France, "Some of Jesus' followers were, and remained, rich and influential men. Joseph of Arimathea does not seem to have felt the need to sell his estate, despite sufficient commitment to Jesus' cause to impel him to defy the Sanhedrin and make a risky appeal to Pilate. Zacchaeus made drastic donations and restitution, but was not apparently required to renounce all his possessions." We could add other New Testament characters like Titus or the Philippian jailor or Lydia the seller of purple. On the other hand Paul (with the exception of his occasional tent making) and his followers seem, like the apostles, to have largely opted out of the economic struggle.

To the question. Was there then a two-tier system of discipleship under which the most fully committed who traveled with Jesus renounced private possessions while a wider circle retained their possessions and so provided the means for the support of the inner circle? France replies, "To a large extent this seems to be the case: there was a distinction between the commitment of those who joined Jesus on a full-time basis and those of his supporters who remained in their homes and job."

France's reply leaves me uneasy. Are there indeed two kinds of commitment that Jesus calls for—or even that he tolerates? Certainly no such idea is found in his teachings. "If any man would come after me, let him deny himself and take up his cross daily and follow me" (Lk. 9:23). "He who does not take up his cross and follow me is not worthy of me" (Mt. 10:38). The claims of Christ on his followers are expressed in various forms, yet always they seem to apply equally to every follower.

Nevertheless there does appear to have been then as now, in economic terms at least, a two-tier system. In this France is right though he himself points out that the distinction was far from absolute. Peter retained his property in Capernaum (Mk. 1:29) and returned briefly to fishing

(Jn. 21:3). It seems (from a comparison of the account of his call and that of the postresurrection fishing) that he retained his boat and equipment.

Yet commitment in economic terms is surely a reflection of commitment in psychological terms, that is, the commitment of our all to the person of Jesus. Are we to suppose that it was Christ's intention for there to be two recognized levels of commitment to him? I do not believe so. While the economic expression of commitment may vary, Christ demands everything of his followers. Commitment is meant to be total. What then should the attitude of his followers be to material possessions? How is commitment to be spelled out in terms of lifestyle and economics?

Treasure in Heaven "Do not lay up for yourselves treasures on earth, where moth and rust consume and where thieves break in and steal, but lay up for yourselves treasure in heaven, where neither moth nor rust consumes and where thieves do not break in and steal. For where your treasure is, there will your heart be also" (Mt. 6:19-21).

"Do not lay up for yourselves treasures on earth. . . ." Is this a command that the followers of Jesus must obey, or is it a recommendation that his followers will do well to adopt? In either case it calls for a radical re-evaluation of our lifestyle. Yet how can we understand the spirit in which our Lord speaks?

Several times in the famous sermon of which these sentences form a part Jesus contrasted heavenly and earthly perspectives. "Love your enemies and pray for those who persecute you, *so that you may be sons of your Father who is in heaven.* . . . Beware of practicing your piety before men in order to be seen by them; *for then you will have no reward from your Father who is in heaven.* ... And when you pray, you must not be like the hypocrites; for they love to stand and pray in the synagogues and at the street corners, that they may be seen by men. Truly, I say to you, they have received their reward. But when you pray, go into your room and shut the door and pray to your Father who is in secret; *and your Father who sees in secret will reward you"* (Mt. 5:44-45; 6:1, 5-6, my emphasis). Repeatedly Jesus shows two radically different ways of viewing things here on earth, the heavenly way and the earthly. If we share one view we will act one way, but if we share the other we will act differently.

Jesus does not seem to exalt poverty. The verse about laying up treasure in heaven is not a command but an appeal to sanctified common sense, or better a challenge to the faith of those who profess to believe in heavenly realities. Clearly, if earthly treasures are corruptible and insecure, we will do better to employ our time securing heavenly treasure. To transpose the recommendation to the twentieth century, if televisions can go on the blink, cars depreciate, fashionable clothes go out of date, if bonds and jewels can be stolen, insurance companies go bankrupt, banks fail, and war and inflation destroy property and the value of money, it would make more sense to devote our energies to accumulating a celestial fortune.

But notice. Jesus sees earthly and heavenly fortune-hunting to be in competition. ("Do not lay up A but lay up B.") We might prefer it to be a question of both/and whereas he seems to see it as either/or—either treasure on earth or treasure in heaven. Apparently we cannot hedge our bets.

But before I follow this idea further let me be practical. Is saving wrong? Should we never make provision for the future? Does the teaching of Jesus open the way to irresponsibility? Where do common sense and prudence end and treasure hoarding and greed begin? Did our Creator not teach squirrels to hoard their nuts for winter?

"The diligent man will get precious wealth," asserts Solomon (Prov. 12:27). "A good man leaves an inheritance to his children's children" (Prov. 13:22). "The soul of the diligent is richly supplied" (Prov. 13:4). We cannot and must not say that prosperity is any more evil than prudence. Nor may we damn the possession of wealth.

The problem begins to arise when we start to ask how far we should go either in making provision for the future or in accumulating things. If Scripture were to do the decent thing and come right out with how much hoarding we should do in the name of responsibility and exactly where the line lay separating prudence from greed, we would find it much easier. But Scripture never does and the Holy Spirit never will. For we are asking the wrong question. If we read the Sermon on the Mount carefully we begin to see that Jesus seems more concerned with the psychology of the thing. Having begun by pointing out that it makes better sense to work for treasures that will last, he immediately adds enigmatically, "For where your treasure is, there will your heart be also" (Mt. 6:21).

We can infer from his statement that only one hoard will in practice constitute treasure. Either it will be the heavenly hoard or the earthly. It cannot be both. We could almost invert the words of Jesus and they would still be true. "Where your heart is, there will your treasure be also." Jesus has redefined *treasure* to mean "that in which I take my greatest delight and toward which I devote my greatest efforts." His interest seems to lie in what treasure means to us and what effect it has on us and particularly in what it does to our capacity to see.

"The eye is the lamp of the body. So, if your eye is sound, your whole body will be full of light; but if your eye is not sound, your whole body will be full of darkness. If then the light in you is darkness, how great is the darkness!" (Mt. 6: 22-23). To have a sound or single eye seems in the context to mean to have a true perspective. So long as we are torn between material things and heavenly things our judgment will be clouded, and we will not be capable of "seeing" matters as God sees them. If on the other hand we are concerned solely with heavenly treasure and cease to worry about collecting material things, matters which previously puzzled us will begin to fall into place. But to be ambivalent is to be confused and uncertain ("full of darkness").

This too is a psychological law. Our goal in life will determine our view of life. We see whatever supports the view we already espouse. Conservative politicians will see those things that confirm their position, as will liberals also. We view life through the tinted spectacles of the philosophy we have already chosen, so that what we see is predetermined by what we are. Butterfield refers to communist and Catholic historians "screaming across interstellar wastes their respective versions of history," each view reflecting a different mental set.

Since God is at the heart of reality, only by seeking him can we wear untinted glasses and begin to see things as he sees them. Our problem, however, is like that of my Cantonese merchant. We would like to believe that our treasure was in heaven and that heaven was our real choice. But the fact is that we find ourselves filled with anxiety. Earthly treasures continue to attract. We may not want outrageous wealth and would be content with reasonable financial security. But we don't want to miss out on anything either. We are ambivalent. We straddle the fence. Even our goal of "reasonable financial security" eludes us perpetually while we try in vain to conjure up a "treasure" feeling toward heaven. We succeed in neither goal but are of all men and women most miserable. We do not possess a single eye and are incapable of willing one thing.

We are like the monkey with his fist trapped inside the coconut shell clutching a fistful of peanuts. The monkey wants freedom and peanuts, and he cannot have both. He must leave the peanuts if he wants to get away. As a matter of fact he will lose both peanuts and freedom if he hangs on too long. And we are caught in a similar bind. We long to be free of earthly entanglements to serve God in the Spirit. Yet we cling to something more elusive than peanuts. We may only want *enough.* But without realizing it we redefine *enough* again and again with the passage of time. Others of us want to have as much as we can get. So we are full of darkness.

"No one can serve two masters; for either he will hate the one and love the other, or he will be devoted to the one and despise the other. You cannot serve God and mammon" (Mt. 6:24). *Mammon* refers to money or to material things. Jesus is talking here as though money were a person, a master controlling the lives of his servants. In the ancient world it was inconceivable that a slave, or for that matter a free servant, should serve two masters. Again, the statement is true psychologically as well. In practice I will find it impossible to be equally devoted to two major goals. One or the other will become nominal and cease to capture my imagination and my fiercest efforts. We cannot devote our hearts and allegiance equally to God and to mammon.

This terrible principle means that so long as mammon fascinates us God does not number us among those who serve him however much "Christian work" we do. We were created to have one center. To try to have two is to be miserable and to enjoy neither spiritual things nor material. It would have been far more pleasant had our consciences never been awakened so as to leave us free to love mammon and mammon alone. As it is we are doomed to dissatisfaction until and unless we slash ourselves free from cords that tie us to mammon or those that bind us to Christ.

The choice for a truly regenerate Christian is a simple one. It lies between the misery of ambivalence and the freedom of valuing Christ, between double darkness and light for the whole body.

If your heart is with the Lord Christ and if you are ardently concerned with the interests of his kingdom, the reasons for the conflict between material possessions and heavenly treasure will become clearer. The more time you devote to meeting with him, worshiping him, learning about him, serving him, the less time you will have available for what is of no value.

The Lord Christ places demands upon his followers which it is their privilege to respond to. His demands differ from those of earthly captains. He insists they let him transform the hours they spend on common tasks—washing, dressing, studying, buying, selling or on working for earthly masters—so that these activities henceforth be performed as acts of worship ardently rendered to his glory. Then he opens new and golden hours that were once vainly wasted so that now they may be devoted to feeding the hungry, clothing the naked, healing the sick, opening the eyes of the blind, comforting the sorrowing and proclaiming his blood-bought liberty for slaves of sin.

Such is the light of glory the Lord Christ sheds on the earthly doings of his followers so that any shoddy garbage surrounding them is seen for what it is. His followers grow sensitive to the evil of the days they live in and begin to redeem the time. Their focus shifts from a material to a heavenly perspective. Slowly they begin to discover that they scarcely have time to acquire the means to procure their daily needs.

"Do not be anxious about your life, what you shall eat or what you shall drink, nor about your body, what you shall put on," their Lord tells them. (And with them he tells us also.) "Is not life more than food, and the body more than clothing?" (Mt. 6:25).

In chapter seven we shall see that it does not matter whether we trust God to supply our needs miraculously even though we have "no visible means of support" or whether we "work for a living." When the claims of the Christ grip us we find we have no choice but to trust him about our needs. However great our wealth, we discover that his amazing commands involve walking a pathway of faith. He reminds us of the birds God cares for and of the lilies and the grass. He asks us whether we are not of greater concern to the Father than they, implying that we are absurd to shrink back in fear when the evidence of his providence surrounds us on every hand. "What shall we eat? What shall we drink? What shall we wear?" He mimics us mockingly, adding scornfully that such panic-filled squeals should come only from the mouths of the godless (Mt. 6:25-32).

He is telling us that God knows we need food and clothing. Presumably he knows about all our other needs. While in this passage he does not promise us riches, he makes it plain that it is absurd that his followers should hang back in doubt and fear.

The Basic Issue Jesus finally makes explicit the basic issue he has been talking around all along. "Men of little *faith*," he calls us (Mt. 6:30). For it is want of faith that makes us opt for earthly rather than heavenly treasure. If we really believed in celestial treasures, who among us would be so stupid as to buy gold? We just do not believe. Heaven is a dream, a religious fantasy which we affirm because we are orthodox. If people believed in heaven, they would spend their time preparing for permanent residence there. But nobody does. We just like the assurance that something nice awaits us *when the real life is over.*

You need only skim superficially over New Testament pages to realize that the focus Jesus has on faith seems to differ from Paul's angle on the same subject. That is not to say that master and follower are in conflict. A moment's thought is enough to see that each has a different question in mind.

"What is it that justifies?" is Paul's question. Faced with false teaching by the circumcision party to the Galatian congregations, false teaching that insisted that Gentile believers be circumcised to fulfill the law of Moses, Paul with two magnificent treatises abolishes from early Christendom any thought that peace with God can be based on anything except faith in Christ. To the question, "What is it that justifies?" there can be but one answer. "Faith in Christ justifies —and faith in Christ alone."

The question Jesus constantly addresses is simpler and more basic. It is, "Is faith present?" "When the Son of man comes," he once mused, "will he find faith on earth?" (Lk. 18:8). He hadn't always found it the first time he came. In his own home town "he did not do many mighty works ... because of their unbelief" (Mt. 13:58). To his humiliated disciples, who asked the reason for their failure to cast a demon out of an epileptic boy, he replied, "Because of your little faith" (Mt. 17:20). After he was raised from the dead, while the same disciples were too disheartened to credit stories of his resurrection, he appeared to them and reproached them for their want of faith (Mk. 16:14).

It is not that Jesus failed to teach justification by faith. While he may not have used the expression, the concept appears more than once in John's Gospel (5:24, for example). Nevertheless the question that seems to lie behind much of his teaching remains, "Where is faith to be found? Is it present here?" Repeatedly he applauds great faith and reproves its absence (such as Mt. 6:30; 8:10, 26; 14:31; 16:8; Mk. 4:40; Lk. 7:9; 12:28).

I said that the question, "Is faith present?" is a simple question, simpler than, "What is it that justifies?" However, we tend to concentrate nowadays on the Pauline question, almost as if we think that by rightly understanding justification by faith we shall automatically possess the faith that justifies. We forget that Melanchthon the scholar taught that very doctrine to Luther the believer, but that as far as we know Melanchthon, whose scholarly genius contributed so much to Luther's Galatian commentary, died an unbeliever. Yet Luther, who had not really grasped the doctrine until at least four years after he had completed his first draft of the Romans commentary (and some years after he nailed his defiant theses to the door in Wittenberg), was justified by faith long before his mind had encompassed the doctrine. It would appear that one may apprehend and even assent to the doctrine without possessing the faith the doctrine speaks of while another who has not yet grasped its content may nonetheless have justifying faith.

Jesus' fundamental question remains then, How can we know when justifying faith is present? How may I know whether it is present in me? Or in Western churches? What test can we apply?

One answer Jesus gives is that faith in the invisible God can be demonstrated by power over material things, either power to manipulate them or power to escape enslavement to them. If someone's life is controlled by material things, it is possible that such a person knows nothing of saving faith. One who could not believe something fundamental in the visible universe cannot be expected to believe spiritual reality. Thus of a perplexed Nicodemus Jesus demands, "If I have told you earthly things and you do not believe, how can you believe if I tell you heavenly things?" (Jn. 3:12). Again when the scribes criticize the way he pronounces forgiveness of sins over a paralyzed man, he asks, "Which is easier, to say to the paralytic, 'Your sins are forgiven,' or to say, 'Rise, take up your pallet and walk'?" (Mk. 2:9). He then proceeded to demonstrate his authority in the invisible realm by showing his power over things visible. The paralyzed man got up. The scribes were obliged to close their mouths, and all who were present praised God for his power.

Let me restate the principle. We must be suspicious of any faith about personal justification that is not substantiated by faith in God's power over material things in our everyday life. Faith about pie in the sky when I die cannot be demonstrated. Faith that God can supply my need today *can* be demonstrated. And if someone claims to possess justifying faith but shows no evidence of it, we may ask such a person whether he or she understands the difference between faith and mental assent. *Enslavement to the visible makes faith in the invisible suspect.*

What did the young ruler need to do in order to gain eternal life and heavenly treasure? He needed to sell all he had and to follow Jesus. But he was unable to (Mt. 19:16-22). Why? Because he loved what he trusted, and he trusted his great possessions. He was a slave of the visible. He lacked effective faith in the invisible God. Had he enjoyed such faith he need not have clung to his riches. He was not damned for possessing them, only for hanging on to them as if they were a lifeboat on a stormy sea.

James also touches the point that clinging to money may indicate the absence of saving faith. "If a brother or sister is ill-clad and in lack of daily food, and one of you says to them, 'Go in peace, be warmed and filled,' without giving them the things needed for the body, what does it profit? So faith by itself, if it has no works, is dead" (2:16-17).

The question behind the teaching of Jesus ("Is faith present?") strikes like a dagger into our chests. Do we have faith? Or do our lives consist only in the abundance of our possessions? Are we enslaved by our possessions?

Security. How we plan for it! We save. We invest. We are provident, responsible. We think of our old age and of our children's educations. Little by little we build our tiny fortresses, hiding from the threat of penury behind savings, locks and bolts. Inflation? Some of us may be worried enough to invest in things we hope inflation will not affect. Others among us smile secretly for we are experienced investors and feel we have solved the problem.

We are like the rich fool. Our professions and businesses have brought forth plentifully. We have more money than we need—even after giving our tithes. What can we do? We discuss matters carefully with our accountants, and having acted on sound advice we tell ourselves, "We now have ample reserves. Let us travel abroad in winter and spend our summers with the children. We have earned it. It is time we took things easy!"

The rich fool (Lk. 12:15-21) was not a fool for harvesting abundant crops. He was a fool for letting his crops fill his horizon and determine his lifestyle. He was a slave to barns and grain, and seems to have had no interest in God. When God's awful voice awakened him from his dreams saying, "Fool! This night your soul is required of you; and the things you have prepared, whose will they be?" he had to leave his barns and enter the Presence naked. Had he sent anything on in advance? Jesus didn't say. Presumably he had forwarded nothing. His heart was back among his mountains of grain.

But notice the conclusions we have reached. The thrust of Jesus' teaching does not deal with the virtues of poverty or the sin of riches. Rather he seeks to show us first the greater value of heavenly treasure and the folly of seeking earthly. Then he warns us of the seductive power of riches, the love of which draws our hearts away from him and renders us incapable of serving him. Finally he upbraids us with the unbelief which underlies our anxiety about our material needs.

The Good of Creation   The desire to possess material things and a love of the things of God are in conflict. This might lead us to suppose that material things are bad and heavenly things good. Is this really so?

Christianity has from time to time been adulterated by teachings wholly alien to it. From its earliest days it was plagued by Gnosticism and by a dualistic view of man and the cosmos. Spirit was what mattered. Our bodies were either essentially evil or else unimportant.

This idea has many forms and still exists under different guises among professing Christians. I suppose we could accuse the Gnostics of being the polar opposites of pragmatic materialists. Instead of declaring that matter is all that matters, some of them might say that spirit is all that matters. Such a view calls for a down playing of the physical creation. Riches, houses, food, sex, forests, mountains, flowers and whatever you like to name are at best irrelevant and at worst evil. Therefore the good consists in a divorce of matter from spirit. This means either I need not concern myself with what my body does (allowing it to indulge itself in any excess for sin also becomes unimportant) or else I deny it any physical gratification in the interests of my spiritual and intellectual development. Thus asceticism is a country cousin of Gnosticism.

Jesus taught us to despise neither our bodies nor material things. There is virtue neither in carelessly indulging our bodies nor in subjecting them to ritual neglect. So Paul in his Colossian letter writes, "If with Christ you died to the elemental spirits of the universe, why do you live as if you still belonged to the world? Why do you submit to regulations, 'Do not handle, Do not taste, Do not touch' (referring to things which all perish as they are used), according to human precepts and doctrines? These have indeed an appearance of wisdom in promoting rigor of devotion and self-abasement and severity to the body, but they are of no value in checking the indulgence of the flesh" (Col. 2:20-23).

The physical universe was created by God. He pronounced it good (Gen. 1:31). Even though it is now tainted by sin, it still reflects his majesty, his beauty, his glory. Matter is not evil, it is only that we have made an evil use of it, becoming idolatrous in our attitude to it, chaining ourselves with gold chains. We have made the good the enemy of the best. We have worshiped the creature rather than the Creator.

Because matter is good, God may reward those he loves with an abundance of it. "And the Lord restored the fortunes of Job . . . and the Lord gave Job twice as much as he had before" (Job 42:10).

Precisely such a reward is mentioned by Jesus in the Sermon on the Mount. "Seek first [God's] kingdom and his righteousness and all these things shall be yours as well" (Mt. 6:31-33). The phrase "all these things" refers to food and clothing. We might call them necessities rather than rewards. The point is that whatever we call them, they are given by the heavenly Father, and therefore must be good things, since he does not give his children evil gifts (Mt. 7: 11). Paul makes matters explicit in his first letter to Timothy when, probably referring to some species of Gnostics he says that they "forbid marriage and enjoin abstinence from foods which God created to be received with thanksgiving by those who believe and know the truth. For everything created by God is good, and nothing is to be rejected if it is received with thanksgiving" (1 Tim. 4:3-4).

We must not combat materialism by embracing the opposite error of asceticism. There is no virtue in poverty unless in the course of our obedience to God we have to endure poverty because of a greater end. Many missionaries endure relative poverty—relative, that is, to what they might have enjoyed (though not to the people they minister to) had they not opted to serve God in foreign missions. Poverty in that case is an occupational hazard. Wise missionaries will accept relative poverty in order not to raise unnecessary barriers between themselves and the people they serve. These missionaries do not exactly embrace poverty. They are (or should be) indifferent to it, content to be poor if being poor facilitates the work being carried out.

Jesus accepted poverty not because it was virtuous but because to save he had to leave heaven's riches to become human. Paul points to Christ's poverty when he exhorts the Corinthian church to give to relief work. "For you know the grace of our Lord Jesus Christ, that though he was rich, yet for your sake he became poor, so that by his poverty you might become rich" (2 Cor. 8:9).

We are not called to imitate Christ's poverty but to follow him in his example of love and self-giving, not caring whether we be poor or rich so long as we follow him and do his will. Should he heap material riches upon us, well and good. But if our lot should be one of pain and penury, we are to laugh at our difficulties, counting them as nothing, "looking to Jesus the pioneer and perfecter of our faith, who for the joy that was set before him endured the cross, despising the shame" (Heb. 12:2). He had contempt for what he underwent. We too, should hardship come upon us, are called to despise it, thinking only of the glory of our task and of our Leader.

The Peril of Wealth   Abundance may or may not represent God's goodness to a man or woman. It may merely indicate industry or the good fortune to inherit riches or that the rich person is a crook. We must never assume that to be wealthy is ipso facto to be in God's good books. There are extremely wicked rich people just as there are godly rich.

A careful reading of the Bible will indicate that the rich are condemned only for the misuse of riches. I mentioned earlier that Christ's concern about material possessions had to do with the effect they have on my relationship with him and on my relationship with my neighbor. Both are present in his recommendation for the rich young ruler. He was to sell all he had in order to give to the poor (that is, to be concerned with his needy neighbor) and to follow Christ (Mt. 19:16-22).

The two relationships go hand in hand. They cannot be separated. For concern for one's neighbor arises out of a true relationship with God. When Jesus was asked to cite "the great commandment" he immediately quoted two. "You shall love the Lord your God with all your heart, and with all your soul, and with all your mind. This is the great and first commandment. And a second is like it, You shall love your neighbor as yourself. On these two commandments depend all the law and the prophets." (Mt. 22: 37-40). Given that upon these two loves (of God and of one's neighbor) hangs all biblical teaching about our duty, it makes sense that God's concern about wealth should focus on how it affects our relationship with him and how it affects our relationship with our neighbor.

These concerns are present in the Old Testament as well as the New. It is sometimes suggested that Amos, to take one example, damned riches in themselves. But this is not so. "For three transgressions of Israel, and for four, I will not revoke the punishment; because they sell the righteous for silver, and the needy for a pair of shoes—they that trample the head of the poor into the dust of the earth, and turn aside the way of the afflicted" (Amos 2:6-7). He speaks of Samaria's rich women as those "who oppress the poor, who crush the needy" (Amos 4:1). The Samaritan rich were exploiters of the poor, and it was against their heartless oppression that the prophet spoke.

Concern for the poor neighbor is evident in the primitive church. In clarifying his relationship with the apostles in Jerusalem, Paul remarks, "They would have us remember the poor, which very thing I was eager to do" (Gal. 2:10). Bad conduct around the Lord's table in Corinth was condemned not primarily because of the drunkenness of the richer members but because of their heartless snobbery. The rich brought food and wine for their social peers, thus cutting themselves off from their poorer brethren and causing division in Christ's body. "When you meet together, it is not the Lord's supper that you eat. For in eating, each one goes ahead with his own meal, and one is hungry and another is drunk. What! Do you not have houses to eat and drink in? Or do you despise the church of God and humiliate those who have nothing? What shall I say to you? Shall I commend you in this? No, I will not" (1 Cor. 11: 20-22).

"Come now, you rich," writes James, "weep and howl for the miseries that are coming upon you. Your riches have rotted and your garments are moth-eaten. Your gold and silver have rusted, and their rust will be evidence against you and will eat your flesh like fire." James speaks prophetically. He looks into the future and sees the terrible judgment that will come upon rich people. But again, is it of being rich that James accuses them? No. "Behold," he continues "the wages of the laborers who mowed your fields, which you kept back by fraud, cry out; and the cries of the harvesters have reached the ears of the Lord of hosts. You have lived on the earth in luxury and in pleasure; you have fattened your hearts in a day of slaughter. You have condemned, you have killed the righteous man; he does not resist you" (5:1-6). The rich wallowed in the luxury of riches they had acquired by paying low wages, by callous indifference to the poor and by flagrant injustice. They could kill and extort because they had power.

Riches are not evil but they are dangerous. Happy are those who are not beguiled by them, for they are few! "Truly, I say to you, it will be hard for a rich man to enter the kingdom of heaven. Again I tell you, it is easier for a camel to go through the eye of a needle than for a rich man to enter the kingdom of God" (Mt. 19:23-24).

Riches corrupt everybody who is in the least corruptible. God is merciful and can deliver the rich from the danger of being rich. But many of us do not want to be delivered. We say we trust God. But we act as though our trust is in riches, as indeed it often is. Riches undermine faith.

We live in a day when those in business (not all of whom are rich) who claim to be born again have facilitated their business relationships by publishing evangelical yellow pages. We could argue about the rights and wrongs of such listings, but what troubles me is to see the name of Christ publicly linked with some businesses that seem to be highly unethical, even though their owners or directors profess to know Christ.

My wife and I prefer to avoid doing business with Christians unless they are personally known to us as trustworthy. Two things concern us. First, we do not want to join the crowd of people who go to such Christians under the impression that by claiming to belong to Christ they can expect a better deal than a non-Christian would get. We also have found from experience that someone in business who professes Christianity is just as likely to give us a dishonest deal as a non-Christian is. Unjust trading and exploitation of employees seem to go together. In saying this I must make it clear that I know Christian businessmen and women who excel both in their competence and their integrity, and who clearly have not sold out to mammon. But there are others who exploit employees and customers alike, and I am filled with shame when I think of them. It is of such that James speaks.

We must leave their judgment to God and possess our souls in patience. We are in no position to condemn people richer than ourselves if we have not known the terrible power of possessions. "Give me neither poverty nor riches," pleaded Agur the son of Jakeh. "Feed me with the food that is needful for me, lest I be full, and deny thee, and say, 'Who is the LORD?' or lest I be poor, and steal" (Prov. 30:8-9).

Corporate Riches   Riches do not only affect us in our personal affairs. They equally affect us in our corporate relationships. Some clubs are snobbish and boast luxurious facilities, pandering to the egos of their members. Beautiful, ornate buildings and facilities do the same. Those of us who do not possess personal riches may gain vicarious satisfaction by belonging to such clubs.

There is a threat of riches corrupting our personal and corporate affairs in church too. We may become spiritual snobs wanting fellowship only with "the right kind" of

Christian people, unconsciously excluding racial minorities or the uneducated, and certainly the down and out. Not only does corporate wealth affect our relations with others, it undermines our faith in God as well as our dependence upon the Holy Spirit. It is chiefly on the effect of riches on our corporate lives as Christians that I shall dwell in succeeding chapters. It only makes sense that its effects on our personal lives will be no different from our corporate life.

If the majority of church members and the members of the governing body have never in their own lives resolved the issue of treasure in heaven, is it not inevitable that their uncertainty will be expressed in the church's policies and outlook? By this I do not mean that the church will cease to proclaim the gospel or to value Scripture. You can preach the gospel for many reasons. You may do so to glorify Christ and because you share his concern for lost sheep. Or you may simply want to swell the congregation, to make your church a winner in the competition of swelling congregations.

What springs first into your mind when you think of your local church? Its buildings and facilities? The pastor? The Sunday morning turnout? The choir? The Sunday school? Or do you think of a body of people with needs and longings?

Where would the earthly Jesus fit into its congregational organization? Do the board members reflect the otherworldly outlook of the apostles? Do members of the congregation concern themselves more with heavenly treasure than with earthly prestige and comfort? Is the pastor concerned more with a building program than with making disciples?

What about you? Let me level with you. I have never

found mammon easy to get away from. While I renounced my allegiance to him many years ago, he continually sends his emissaries to tempt me. My ears are often deafened by the noise of his propaganda while my eyes swim with the attractive pictures he paints. When it comes to the crunch I know which side I'm on, and I try to make a right decision, but I cannot say the decision is always painless. At times I have to opt for heavenly treasure in the teeth of my yearning to possess. But I am grateful that I experience increasing liberty as I choose Christ.

There may be no point in your reading further in this book unless you have given serious thought to your personal priorities. The book assumes that material things corrupt. Unless you are so convinced of this that you opt for heaven, whatever the decision may cost you, then your concern for the church's materialism will not lead to change.

I cannot quote admonitions to rich churches in the New Testament since there do not seem to have been any rich churches. Paul told the Corinthian Christians, who seemed to think highly of themselves, "For consider your call, brethren; not many of you were wise according to worldly standards, not many were powerful, not many were of noble birth; but God chose what is foolish in the world . . . what is weak . . . what is low and despised" (1 Cor. 1:26-28). The Corinthians may not have had material riches to count on but they seemed to be worldly rather than heavenly in their outlook.

The first hint of corporate riches comes in our Lord's epistle to the loathesomely lukewarm church at Laodicea. "For you say, I am rich, I have prospered, and I need nothing; not knowing that you are wretched, pitiable, poor, blind, and naked" (Rev. 3:17). Material riches had cooled their ardor as it cools the spiritual ardor of many a modern congregation.

The most terrifying effect of Christian corporate riches is that faith in God is substituted by business know-how and dependence on technical methodology.

Many years ago I stood one night in the rain, looking wonderingly at the walls of what was then the China Inland Mission headquarters in London. I had read many C.I.M. books, including the two-volume biography of Hudson Taylor, and had been thrilled and quickened by the way God had supplied the mission's needs "through prayer to God alone" (which I discuss more in chapter seven).

That night as I looked at the dirty but solid brick wall I reached out my hand to touch it. It seemed like a holy thing. Not that the C.I.M. was anything other than a human organization blessed and used by God. But to me the walls were an awesome and tangible monument to the reality of God's response to faith. It was as though God himself had put them there. "This is what God did," I said, glowing warmly, feeling the solidity of the wet bricks as awe stole over my whole body. "A solid monument to God's response to faith."

There are many so-called monuments to faith around the world today. People would like us to believe that God raised them in answer to believing prayer. I don't think so. Many are monuments to human ingenuity, to public relations know-how, to clever advertising, to skill in milking Christian suckers. And since we would not need to depend on public-relations know-how and clever advertising if we truly believed in God, I suppose it is correct to say that the buildings of which I speak are monuments to unbelief rather than monuments to faith. We view them with understandable (but culpable) pride. We have made it. We need nothing.

May God have mercy on us! For we are wretched, pitiable, poor, blind and naked.

5

THE GOLDEN COW

In his role as the last and great prophet Jesus warned his followers about forgetting to whom they belonged and of selling themselves to mammon. Against commercialized desecration of the Temple he acted violently, expressing the same moral reprehension that inspired earlier prophets to call God's people a whore.

The twentieth-century church has also forgotten which master she belongs to, painting herself like a hussy in her silly pursuit of Lord Mammon. Or, to use another image, the church has gone a-whoring after a golden cow.

Not a calf, if you please, but a cow. I call her a *golden* cow because her udders are engorged with liquid gold, especially in the West where she grazes in meadows lush with greenbacks. Her priests placate her by slaughtering godly principles upon whose blood she looks with tranquil satisfaction. Anxious rows of worshipers bow down before their buckets. Although the gold squirts endlessly the worshipers are trembling lest the supply of sacrificial victims should one day fail to appease her.

I used to be angry with my fellow fundamentalists and outraged at certain evangelical institutions because of their materialistic attitudes. But my rage has long since subsided. I even went through a charitable and patronizing stage. May God forgive me. Who am I to rage or to patronize?

I know some children whose mothers are whores. Can you imagine what it feels like to discover your mother goes to bed with men for money? In point of fact such children feel a variety of emotions, ranging from indifference to bitter rejection to shame to (occasionally) hurt mingled with compassion. It's hard to quit loving your own mother, even if she is a whore. You've only got one.

Fundamentalism is my mother. I was nurtured in her warm bosom. She cared for me with love and taught me all she knew. I owe her (humanly speaking) my life, my spiritual food and many of my early joys. She introduced me to the Savior and taught me to feed on the bread of life. Our relationship wasn't all honey and roses, but she was the only mother I had. I clung to her then and find it hard not to lean on her now. If she let me down at times I'm old enough to realize that no mother is perfect. But to find out that she was a whore, that she let herself be used by mammon, was another matter. And as the wider evangelical movement gradually took her place in my life it was painful to make the same discovery twice.

Yet we are still family. I am still a part of the evangelical movement. We are, as it were, of the same flesh and blood.

Collective Responsibility   In the last chapter I referred to the way riches affect us corporately. We bear a collective responsibility for the worship I refer to even though as individuals some of us may believe we worship only the one true God. There were many prophets who had not bowed the knee to Baal in Elijah's day, yet all Israel suffered the seven-year drought.

Wide differences in practice and in attitudes characterize different Christians so that when I make a generalization it may seem unfair. Yet in ways God holds us, I believe, collectively responsible for what goes on among us. We draw away from one another into distinct groups and church organizations indulging in the liberty this gives us to criticize another group as though we ourselves had no connection with it. We are obsessed by the individualism of the culture we live in. Yet in Christ we are one body. Shall one eye say to the other, "Poor toe, she's got cancer"? When I make a generalization, then, I make it with the full awareness of the wide differences that exist and with the hope that we will not all delight in a false liberty to point fingers while remaining immune from guilt ourselves.

Let me expand, too, on what I mean by worshiping the golden cow. Is mass advertising wrong? Is it wrong for Christian groups to be concerned with their relations with the public? Without giving the matter much thought I would answer no to both questions, but the questions themselves are naive.

No, when I talk about worshiping the golden cow, I am talking about a particular form of materialism to which we have fallen prey. It is a way of life that sets our feet on the road to spiritual harlotry. And I think it will be better for me to describe the materialistic way of life I refer to rather than define it. I may succeed in showing how and why we have become materialists and that we bear more than a collective guilt. For while it is true that Christian institutions follow such ritual forms of worship as mass advertising and public relations techniques, they would never do so if the rest of us were not also guilty at heart of a greed for *things*.

Salesmen: Priests of the New Worship If you were to ask what kind of person typifies the twentieth century, I think many people's minds would flash to astronauts. Yet the person who expresses the spirit of our age more than any other is not the astronaut but the salesman.

Most of us live lives far removed from space platforms. Our days are spent earning money to pay for the cars we bought, and our evenings and weekends to spending more money, the money we hope to earn tomorrow. Our grasping arms are being crammed with the produce of an age of abundance, our eagerness to grasp being more than matched by the zeal of the people who would shower such produce upon us. Abundance in the West has become a menace threatening to inundate us under mountains of television sets, houses, clothes, flowery toilet paper, cars, snowmobiles, books, furniture. In order that we may avoid being deluged, goods must be "kept moving." Advertising has been carried to lengths never before known. Our mailboxes, telephones, radios and televisions are channels for would-be sellers of merchandise who are hard put to get rid of what the manufacturers produce.

There is nothing wrong, of course, with a proper distribution of goods and services. I am not talking about that but about the promotion of superabundance. We need food, clothing and shelter. Even abundance and comfort are gifts of God. But we are no longer his creatures accepting and distributing the goodness he pours upon us but the feverish and slavish worshipers of abundance itself.

So the sound of your doorbell may herald the Fuller Brush man or the Avon lady. The ring of the telephone may precede slick patter from a bogus researcher or an invitation to a party where anything from wigs and coffee to Tupperware and tea lend an air of friendly neighborhood fun to the deadly business of keeping the economy expanding. If we leave our homes, we still cannot escape for our eyes are assailed by billboards and our ears by commercials on the car radio. (It sometimes amuses me to speculate that the most prized art of an age to come may be a twentieth-century television commercial.)

The life force of the vast and complex sales organization is an army of sales representatives, varying widely in background, training and ethical standards. Some are college graduates; others never finished grade school. Some fly first class and enter into delicate negotiations with city halls, state legislatures and directors of companies. Others trudge from door to door in suburbia or sit with a telephone book in their lap dialing numbers. Some are conscientious and have high ethical standards. Others are grubby shysters. Yet their goal is a common one: to sell you and me as much of their company's produce as they can. They are the priests of the god of greed.

When you ask sales reps how they view their method of earning a living, they may tell you that they are carrying out a public service. Their function is to find what your need is and to meet it. It is not in their interest or yours (they will say) to foist on you a product you neither need nor want. And in performing a service for you, they are not only helping you by providing a product but themselves by gaining a commission. The more their company can profit from sales, the greater will be its growth and therefore its ability to bring prosperity to the whole community. (And prosperity, remember, means more abundance all round.) In competing with sales of inferior articles they are also helping to improve standards. Inferior articles become extinct monsters in a sort of survival of the commercially fittest.

All of us recognize that bad salesmen and women, bad in the moral sense, exist. But equally we recognize that there are good ones, good in the sense that they do not allow their urge to clinch a sale to override their sense of fairness to the customer. Chambers of commerce as well as organizations such as the Christian Businessmen's Committee exist among other things to promote more ethical business practices (though how successful they are in doing so is cast in doubt by the growth of consumer organizations).

But what of the system of which sales people are so vitally a part? If we shift our perspective for a moment, we shall see that far from being the central character in the twentieth-century drama, the sales representative in turn is but a puppet manipulated by more powerful hands. Indeed we may see more still. We shall see if we look hard enough that the system could not operate apart from human greed, the greed all of us share.

Let us look then at the system's use of advertising. Does modern advertising really help manufacturers meet society's need by making us all aware of how and where our needs can be met? Or do advertising and sales people, in the complex sales structure of which they form a part, trade on our greed by creating artificial needs so as to market unneeded products? They probably do both, but their real prosperity lies in doing the latter.

The Cow Is a Cheat   Social critics have for some years been decrying advertisers. Many have attacked not only North America's rigid social system but an economy based on forced obsolescence. Disturbing questions are being asked.

How does one define *need* in a society where standards of living are constantly rising? Are electric can openers *necessary* in any sense of the word? What is to be said of our sense of values when millions of dollars were invested in making and marketing them at a time when people in India were concerned with keeping themselves and their children from starvation? How *necessary* is flowered underwear for men or any other change of fashion in cars, houses, clothes or bathroom faucets? How about the "need" for shifting hemlines up or down? Or TV dinners?

Again, how do the generals of the sales army in their carpeted offices on Madison Avenue plot their strategy for meeting our "needs"? What angles do they play on besides our greed? Our anxieties? (Is your family protected?) Our sexual preoccupations? (Does your breath rob you of kisses?) Our guilt? Our snobbery? (You deserve the best.)

Is it right that society gain prosperity from cigarette sales at the cost of people gasping and coughing with lung cancer? Or by liquor commercials when others die of liver failure? How do we view a system that is upheld, at least in part, by a calculated appeal to our psychological weaknesses?

And having asked such critical questions about mass advertising, what are we saying about ourselves, especially about ourselves as Christians? What kind of blind fools are we to be duped by the worship of the god of greed? Do we really believe his promises to give us happiness? And if we say we don't, why do we pour out our money in offerings to him? If you think a little more about it you will begin to see that the sales people, the advertisers and all of us who fall for their ploys are deceived victims of the same god who will ultimately destroy us all.

Take sales reps again. How fair is the system to them? What about the rosy pictures painted for them at sales conventions? Is it fair to "psych-up" people who never could and never will make their fortune (or even their living) in selling, so as to squeeze a few more ounces out of their mediocre potential? It may benefit the company and perhaps the economy too, but what about those who in middle age are slowly beginning to realize that the beautiful mirage that fired their enthusiasm is the creation of false prophets of a commercial religion? Are sales representatives priests of a phony religion, or are they donkeys led on by dangling carrots?

Some years ago Arthur Miller wrote a play entitled *Death of a Salesman*. Willie Loman (the salesman) is movingly portrayed in middle age as a bewildered and pathetic man struggling against odds to preserve the dream of a life that was to be. Because of urban development, his home "in the country" is, by the time he has paid for it, dwarfed by high-rise apartments. It is impossible to view him in any other way than as a victim. His suicide, and the questions it raises for all of us, are more than good drama. Throughout Europe, the Western Hemisphere, East Asia, indeed everywhere except perhaps in some Communist countries, thousands of Willie Lomans set out with shining eyes only to encounter eventual disenchantment, alcoholism or the acceptance of living a life of failure.

The god of greed is a cheat. His promise of material rewards may never even be kept. He cheats his priests as much as he cheats his worshipers, turning his back on both and leaving them to their despair once he no longer has use for them. And even those upon whom he lavishes his rewards find them strangely flat. His flowers are made of plastic and his food of sawdust while his wine can neither refresh nor intoxicate. His delights have the power to dazzle and excite but they can satisfy nobody.

I hope I have made it clear that in labeling salespeople and advertising copywriters as priests and prophets of the golden cow I am not singling them out as the heart of the evil system. They may exemplify it, or even symbolize it, but they are not in any sense the key to it. Unless you grasp this you will mistake my writing for a sociological treatise knocking big business and the free-enterprise system. It is too easy to present the capitalists, the bankers, the industrial tycoons as the villains of the piece even though there may be some justice in doing so. Yet if they (as many people tell us) exploit us, do we not make their task all the easier because we are selfish and greedy?

And how do we regard the growth of consumer organizations? Righteousness is on their side, you tell me, but I will answer that greed is in their hearts also. Their cause, and I will concede the point, is a just one. The prophets themselves denounced wealthy oppressors of the poor. Yet I cannot escape the feeling that all of us—producers, consumers, employers, employees, industrialists, trade unions and advertisers—are tarred with the same brush. I get exactly the same acquisitive feelings rising in me whether I read *The*

Wall Street Journal or *Financial Post* or *Consumer Reports.*

Sponges Soaked with Society's Values   What does it all boil down to? It comes to this: we Christians are too often like sponges soaked to capacity with the value system of the society we live in. Whether we sympathize with labor or industry, whether we are Republicans, Democrats, conservatives, liberals, socialists or whatever, our value systems in practice are one. We may argue fiercely with one another but we base our arguments on the same premise: the greatest good in life is a bigger (or better-cooked) slice of this world's pie, a pie to which we all have an inalienable right.

And it is precisely here, in our unconscious acceptance of a false value system (with its confusion about our "rights") that the root of the problem lies. Here lies the weakness that makes us prone to spiritual harlotry. For we have overvalued material prosperity and have underestimated, taken for granted or even forgotten the God of power and love we profess to worship. We claim to have faith in him. But so long as we are harassed by anxiety about our financial security or overly impressed by the importance of money in Christian work, our profession is hollow and our footsteps follow the pathway to whoredom.

I can claim no immunity to such wrong values. I am myself the kind of sucker who avidly reads a get-rich-quick book. I anxiously weigh the pros and cons of pension schemes versus investment in real estate as hedges against inflation. And why? It is because I too breathe the air full of the incense offered to the cow. So far as I (the carnal I) am concerned, the Sermon on the Mount can cheerfully be relegated to the Kingdom Age. I am by no means sure that it is safe to take no anxious thought for tomorrow. What guarantee is there that seeking first the kingdom of God and his righteousness will mean that "all these things" will be added unto me? Is there no fine print under the guarantee?

But here I blame the churches. Where are the preachers who expound to me these Scriptures? Dispensationalists and nondispensationalists can agree or disagree on the hermeneutics of Matthew 6. But I believe the real reason we avoid such passages or hedge them with words like *but, mind you, on the other hand,* and *we must always bear in mind* has nothing to do with dispensational theology. It is due to our secret worship of the cow.

Let the preachers remind the church again that no one can serve two masters! Never mind the congregation members who get sore and defensive. Let us tell men and women that *you cannot serve God and mammon* even in the Church Age.

Let us hammer the message home in churches all over the West. Let us raise from the pulpit the practical issues in our own cities, the neighborhoods of our own churches. City hall will never solve the problems of the downtown poor. Political skullduggery and the abuse of welfare do not excuse us from finding those to whom we can become neighbors. Let us appoint church committees composed of Christian welfare workers, social workers and journalists to assess the needs in our own areas and to make specific recommendations by which we (without city hall) may take the lead in promoting social reform.

At least a part of the church is being made in the image of Western materialism. The tragic outcome of this is a movement which often uses the preaching of the gospel as a means of organizational self-aggrandizement.

A few knees have not bowed down before the golden cow, but they are growing fewer. I am writing with the hope that my words will encourage the few that are left and persuade while there is time the many who are wavering between God and green dollars.

6

PROPERTY AND PAYOLA

If our harlotry were private, if we were to worship the gods of materialism in the secrecy of our hearts or even of our households, the matter would be bad enough. But it is inevitable that, blinded as we are to our error, we have molded our churches by the values that govern our own lives.

We remain blind while the whole world can see what we are doing. We sleep the sleep of the just. Do we not proclaim that eternity matters more than time and the spirit more than body? Do we not urge one another to give to the work of our Lord? Do we not render tithes and offerings?

The Stones Cry Out   We preach and we parade to ourselves. The world ignores our pious performances. The stones of our lovely buildings cry out to the passers-by while the voices from our pulpits remain muffled and dead. The stones are boasting, "We are the symbols of Christ today. Look at us if you want to know what Christians care about."

They are telling the truth. We care very much about them. It seems we argue more heatedly about real estate than we ever do about doctrine. In fact sometimes when we appear to be arguing about doctrine we are actually arguing about control of lands, funds and buildings.

Some years ago when I applied for membership in an evangelical church, one of its leaders mentioned to me the importance the privileges of membership would give me. He stressed the necessity that my application and my doctrinal beliefs be properly screened. Because I thought of membership in terms of fellowship, of discipline and of prayer I promptly concurred. My friend (a warm Christian) cut me short.

"Your words could carry a lot of weight and there are hundreds of thousands of dollars tied up in this property," he told me. "The way you vote could influence the way many other people vote."

I was astounded and begged him to clarify his statement. But as he went on talking, there could be no doubt about it. At that point he was viewing me not just as a brother in Christ but as a potential financial power in the church. I do not believe that my friend's attitude (shocking as it may seem to some people) was anything extraordinary. For the basic issue when you reach rock bottom in many church quarrels is who gets control of the real estate.

Christian groups of all kinds are far too *thing* centered. It is very easy to raise money for a project when the project has something tangible (like a clinic building, a school or a mobile gospel unit with a portable movie screen to show gospel films in villages, and so on) especially if the project has a sentimental or a romantic appeal. People give to something that looks good in a picture. But to find the money to pay a pastor a reasonable wage is all too difficult.

Because Christian organizations are property centered their program becomes property bound. Once you have bought an expensive building (or boat or plane), you have to justify its existence. The argument that prevails when plans are made runs like this: "Well, it seems to me, brother, that we've got a wonderful plane costing thousands of dollars and we're only using it once a month. . . ." So a missionary operation, for example, begins to center round planes, boats, buildings.

Planes, boats and buildings are all of value, but too often they are (without our realizing it) our masters rather than our servants. They sit on our boards and committees and cast their silent votes on every motion.

People tell me it is impossible to go without things. "How could we run our missionary society without buildings and equipment? We would be crippled without them." Exactly. Because the program has become geared to things, it cannot possibly survive without things. And because Western Christian mentality tends to think in terms of things, it can conceive no other way to operate.

Nor is this all. We like to think that our evangelistic and church-building endeavors are planned prayerfully with ultimate goals in view. Not so. They are governed more by the mass psychology of church members than by prayerful planning. Why do I say this? I say it because ordinary church members respond to what they can understand. And they understand things. If you can link in their minds the conversions of Indians with a plane or if you can persuade them of the value that owning a hotel will have for training evangelists, you will open their billfolds.

And the bigger the operation the better. Be they rich or poor, the effect on them will be the same. As they realize that their few dollars will provide a springboard for a massive evangelistic assault, they grow intoxicated with wonder. Money from people all around them pours into Operation Big Deal.

The phrases *God has supplied* and *God has opened the way* are pious phrases that too often mean, "There's more money available for this sort of project, so that's what we'd better do." Consequently the projects that bloom, or at least that create the illusion of blooming, are determined by what most appeals to those who have the least experience in Christian work as money is given in response to the manipulations of Christian entrepreneurs. In the days of Joe McCarthy any Christian radio program knocking communism hit paydirt for Christ. The consequences on Christian work itself are not quite so serious as it might at first appear; the real evil lies in our attitude.

In the Long Run Church-building committees work on a principle which has much to commend it: spending a little more money initially will save later. For example, a paneled wall will never need painting and "will always look good." If anyone criticizes the expenditure on the ground that churches should be helping the poor or the missionaries and be less concerned with the building, the reply runs, "Yes, but we'll actually be *saving* money. If we have to help the poor or the mission field, *in the long run* we'll be able to give them more."

"In the long run." When will that be? What happens to

the needy in the meantime? And do we seriously suppose that the best way to help the poor is for us to use expensive building materials?

There are other pseudoprofundities that cause us all to nod our heads in solemn agreement. "It really represents a saving." "Nothing is too good for God." "People are attracted to nice buildings." (What sort of people? Street-walkers? Welfare recipients? Skid-row bums? Whom do we *wish* to attract?) "We mustn't give the impression that the Christian message is cheap." And so on and so on.

Jesus was accused of eating with publicans and sinners. More than one immoral woman felt at ease in his presence. The poor thronged around him. He had come, he said, to preach the gospel to them.

But we, his modern followers, have sealed ourselves in middle-class, religious ghettos. By our dress, our hair styles, our church buildings, we have raised impenetrable psychological barriers around us, effectively shutting out many who need our redeemer.

Yet if I leave the impression that there is something wrong with good church buildings, I have failed to make my point clear. It is not *possessing* riches that God condemns, but clinging to them, coveting them and having our activity centered around them. It is our wrong way of looking at things, our wrong scale of values, that matters. It is not meeting in a good building that is wrong, but making such a building a priority and fooling ourselves into believing that we can't get on without it. It is building with unnecessary luxury at a time when inequity abounds, thinking more of the building than of the church, more of a good organ than of praise, more of the communion table than the body and blood of Christ. It is worshiping the golden cow.

"Ah, I'm so glad he got round to making this important distinction," someone whispers. "That means we needn't feel guilty about our very fine property and such a *functional* building."

But hold on. There are quite a few churches like yours in lower-middle-class and middle-class sectors in your city. What is going on among the poor? Among the recent immigrants? Among the motley international groups of newcomers struggling to gain a foothold on the lower end of the economic ladder? Do we relegate them all to the ministries of the nineteenth-century downtown missions? Or do we take some responsibility ourselves?

How necessary are the costly facilities of the "functional" structures we have created? How important is it that our young people play volleyball in an "adequate gymnasium"? How necessary is that beautiful Christian education wing? Who from the congregation would be willing to play volleyball with Puerto Ricans or Poles on a vacant downtown lot? Or begin Sunday-school classes in the dreary tenements that surround it? I understand a certain reluctance lest "our young people" be exposed to that sort of thing. I also understand that the denizens of the downtown nether world would feel thoroughly out of place in our luxurious facilities. So what should we do?

I can think of two suggestions. The first would be for the leadership of the church to meet and prayerfully consider the church's responsibilities to neglected areas such as those I have mentioned. Surely God could place a burden on someone's heart for them. Could there not be a prayerful laying on of hands of some who are called to minister elsewhere? To research specific areas and talk to those who know about them? To raise autonomous home fellowships?

The Church of the Redeemer in Houston is only one of many possible models.

My second suggestion is to the expanding church, the church that plans to build "a more adequate facility." My advice is don't. There is the constant argument that "it's always cheaper in the long run to own your own" plane or house, rather than to rent it. Owning your own transportation gets you someplace faster and more conveniently. I shall refer later to a young missionary urging a middle-aged veteran jungle evangelist to go to a faraway jungle village by plane rather than by Indian dugout. "You could be there in an hour," he pleaded. "The way you are going you'll take days—four days cooped up in a canoe with five Indians. Think of all the time you could save."

Churches should rethink priorities. Can downtown facilities be rented for public meetings? Can home study groups become heavenly leaven changing the nature of the core area? Can imaginative schemes be thought up to attract the youth of the area? If so, let your congregation divide. Let those who feel comfortable in your present facility stay there. Let the rest move out to reach the downtrodden.

I must warn you of course to beware of naivité as much as of condescension. But you won't remain naive long. And real love and respect for people leave no room for condescension.

As for our private wealth and our lovely homes, there are many things we can do. We can see that the "guest room" has a higher occupancy rate. We can set up a church organization through which a distress-alert system brings us the abandoned wives and other temporarily distressed persons so that they can find their feet and start life anew themselves. We can invite such needy souls not as guests to whom we show gracious hospitality but as full members of the family who share its joys, its sorrows, its prayers, its celebrations and its day-to-day tasks. Our carpets will get worn faster. Our chesterfields will begin to sag sooner. Our favorite records will get scratched. But since when were we called to live for carpets, chesterfields and stereos?

And how about cars? I just made the discovery that it takes me ten minutes longer to get to work by bus than by car. So now we're a one-car family (still in a luxury class to be sure, for one car is way above one bicycle) and that saves us in Canada around $100 monthly. In how many more ways can we free up money for those in need?

I am deliberately sidestepping the question of whether constructing a beautiful building might not itself be an act of worship to God. I do so not because the question is unimportant but because it is irrelevant. We do not in fact build beautiful buildings from a spirit of worship but for prestige and pride.

Payola for Pastors   Our corporate materialism is seen not only in our attitude to buildings and facilities of every kind, but also in our attitude to pastors and Christian workers.

I meet many pastors. To some I give instruction in pastoral counseling, and others I treat as patients. Often as we have talked together the matter of materialism comes up. Some pastors confess they have to battle a materialistic spirit in themselves, finding that they, too, are influenced by a materialistic culture.

Most of them agree with me that their congregations are too *thing* centered. Some confess to feelings of resentment as they observe members of the congregation growing rich while they themselves make little or no material advance. Their problem is not simply one of covetousness but of feeling forsaken. It seems to many of them that members of their congregation are too busy making money to care deeply enough about the spiritual responsibilities of entering into the pastor's struggles. Occasionally a pastor may actually be told, "That's the sort of thing we pay *you* to do."

It is unwise to generalize, for certainly many Christians are active in their local churches. But too many pastors get the feeling of being paid to run a kind of Christian club. Sunday-school teachers and others who help with the program are like volunteer workers who know little of the agony and pain of pastoral burdens. Their main concern is often that the pastor doesn't show enough interest in *them*.

I occasionally come across a pastor who looks on his salary as thirty pieces of silver. "They are giving me money," he will say, "so they can excuse themselves from a spiritual burden God would lay on their shoulders. And like a Judas I take it." While a few pastors luxuriate in high salaries, others battle with resentments over poor wages. To ask for more money after preaching a sermon on self-sacrifice would be impossible. Yet why, the pastor feels, should he take the major spiritual burden while receiving inadequate pay so others can be set free to make their piles?

Some pastors, as I mentioned, are generously paid and grateful for it. Others moonlight to make ends meet and feel guilty about doing so. Yet others (for greedy pastors exist, some of them nothing more than religious psychopaths) cheat on expenses, manipulate the mission funds or hint about their needs to rich old ladies.

Many, saddened at heart and burdened with a sense of failure, are leaving the pastorate. They feel frustrated, spiritually empty, lonely and bewildered by a schizophrenic sensation of being looked up to in spiritual matters and looked down on in the area that really counts, that of financial success.

For money in our culture is a mark of greatness. If you can grumble about taxes, put a large check in the offering and buy a mink coat, then you are someone indeed. From the pulpit the pastor may look down on the materialism of the rich. But making a pastoral call, he eyes his brother's beautiful suit and his own ill-fitting one, and suddenly feels cheap. He tells himself that treasure in heaven is what matters, but the words no longer bring him comfort.

Partner or Employee? It is easy for people who have not stood where a pastor stands to accuse him of "being defeated." The question is not *whether* he is defeated but why. Who are we to demand that one man in our midst be paid to stand in spiritual isolation? With our words and our handshakes we tell him we are "with him all the way." But by our actions we let him know quite clearly that we have other more important matters to attend to. We are not his partner. He is our paid employee. And we are sometimes proud that we treat our employee so generously.

When every aspect has been considered, what matters most to a good pastor is not the size of the sum he receives but what that money means. If he senses it expresses loving concern and a desire to share freely with him, he may feel like a millionaire. But if it is payola to keep him tactful toward prominent church members or that obliges him to recognize his position as the paid hireling of the church board, then he is abjectly poor, however large his salary.

How in fact should one decide on a pastor's salary? There

is no simple answer. But if you are serious about it, you must address more questions to yourself. Do you need a pastor at all? Some churches don't. (If twenty members gave two and a half hours a week to doing what the pastor is paid to do, they would contribute fifty hours a week.) Why do we not have the time? Is it because money matters to us? Is it in fact *cheaper* to hire a pastor to do God's work?

I know very well that twenty people giving two and a half hours are not the same as one man giving fifty, but that is beside the point. Churches often hire pastors for the wrong reasons, reasons that are rarely admitted. One is that too few actually *believe* the Holy Spirit can weld the church members into a living, active body. The Holy Spirit can only work properly when you hire a pastor. Another reason is the one I have already dealt with: we are too busy making money to give the time God would have us give. Do not misunderstand me. I am not arguing against the pastoral office but pointing to its abuses and the ways in which materialism has corrupted the relationship between pastor and flock.

If you are sure you need a pastor, and you have decided the basic principles by which he should be paid (for example, the number of children he has; what his car and housing allowance are worth; what the median income of the church members is), how do you fix the sum? Again I can only supply you with more questions. If you find yourself getting hung up about money, are you thinking more about money than about the pastor?

What would be wrong with giving him fifty per cent more than whatever sum seems reasonable? Are you afraid it might make *him* too money conscious? If so, what business did you have in appointing him? If you are in a position to pick a pastor, you should also know that God expects you to discern whether he has a weakness about money. And if he has a weakness about money, you should never have given him the responsibility of a pastorate (1 Tim. 3:3)!

Some churches like to give high salaries because the pastor's standard of living will affect the kind of people who will attend. (Posh pastor; fancy congregation.) God is concerned with motives not with amounts. Do you resent the thought of your pastor having too much money? Then double his salary! Why! To show him you love him. But aren't there better ways of showing love? Of course there are, but why not show him love in these ways too? Do you ask me what happens if the salary is too much for him? I answer, that's the pastor's problem. He could give more money away, for instance. Pray that he may have wisdom in handling what he doesn't need.

My cynicism makes me realize that the only real difficulty to arise if we doubled all our pastors' salaries would be an increase in the number of would-be pastors. Yet if we were to deal with the deadly disease of our materialism, the problem of having too many pastors around would be a minor one. (Money is a screen to pick out "spiritual" pastors—double standard.)

Double Standards   Throughout the discussion on pastors' salaries I have been avoiding what may be the crux of the matter. We have the inarticulate feeling that people in Christian work *ought* to live more sacrificially than the rest of us. By and large they do. There are wide disparities within each group I shall refer to, and I can only make a rough generalization. But we could say that in order of financial prosperity, ordinary Christians stand at the top of the heap, pastors next, then home mission workers of various sorts, foreign missionaries from the mainline denominations and finally missionaries from the older (especially European) interdenominational mission groups.

And we are satisfied with the arrangement. This is the way it should be. After all, missionaries are the most spiritual people among us, with pastors next and the rest of us just plain Christians. It sounds absurd when the words are articulated, but I have talked to too many Christians to be fooled. We feel uncomfortable when it is spelled out, but this is the way we actually see it. In fact even when I spell it out, some Christians seem surprised that I see anything wrong with the view.

The most glaring error lies in the assumption that God has two standards of living—one for "full-time" Christians and another for "part-time," volunteer Christians. For this is what the matter boils down to. The expression *full-time worker* is dangerously misleading, implying that while all of us are Christians all the time, only some of us work for God all the time.

The first danger lies in an artificial separation between the sacred and the secular. For Christians no such separation should exist. Brother Lawrence swept the floor for God. Whatever we do ("in word or deed") must be done for him under his Spirit's direction. It must be done out of love for God and aimed at glorifying him. Christians should be those who wipe their noses, clean their teeth, fold their dirty linen, write reports, sell merchandise, play the piano and clean the toilet bowl as acts of worship and service to God. It is no more holy to preach an evangelistic sermon than it is to play catch with the children. What makes these actions holy or otherwise is the attitude of heart from which they spring.

But there is a second danger. Once we have accepted the

full-time/nonfull-time dichotomy we are let off the hook spiritually. It is all very well to talk about being yielded to the Holy Spirit every moment of the day, but we can never be yielded when we accept the idea of a double standard. Say what we like about our dedication. As long as we think of a missionary as being (by virtue of being "full-time") more dedicated than ourselves, we will automatically set limits on what God demands of us. Only by becoming a missionary can we achieve the ultimate in dedication. Thus (so long as we believe this) we will live a less dedicated life than a missionary. And this is nonsense.

The double standard shows up in our materialism, however. We measure spirituality by doing without. Like any false notion, the idea is a half-truth. Jesus left riches in glory and embraced poverty that we might be made rich. He calls us to forsake all we have to follow him.

Notice two things. First, he calls *all* of us to forsake all and follow him. Just as there is no division between those who do sacred and those of us who do secular work, so none exists between groups who are supposed to give up everything to follow him and those of us who are merely to give tithes and offerings. And if for a moment I may set aside the practical difficulty about how we are all supposed to go about giving up all we possess, I must hasten to insist again that we have no right to demand of Christian workers a standard we do not follow ourselves. There is one standard of sacrifice applying equally to every child of God. No one is exempted from it. Any of us who claims to be exempt denies the righteous claims of Christ on his or her life.

Second, to give up everything for Christ consists of an *internal* relinquishment of all our possessions. I have covered the matter in *The Cost of Commitment*. The standard set before us is not that all Christians take a vow of poverty. Some of us will always be richer and others, poorer. Yet all of us are to have a contract with Christ that whenever obedience to him means sacrifice of any degree, even to losing everything we have or to facing prison and death, then obedience is what matters. The obedience will be all the easier if we daily relinquish to him all we possess.

All Christians are called to be disciples. All Christians at any time, under any circumstances are to be ready for new sets of instructions from headquarters which might mean total material loss. So if obedience means that I move to a city where I will make less money or lose my beautiful house, I move, whether I am a missionary or an "ordinary Christian."

It is not that riches, nice homes or luxuries of any kind are in themselves bad. They may in fact represent gifts of a loving God, given for our enjoyment. They have their dangers of course. We get too used to them, too fond of them. Or they can become goals to be achieved. But in themselves they are in no way evil. If our attitude is right we shall inevitably, as I pointed out earlier, share our good homes with those in need of shelter, provided our churches are properly organized to spot and remedy human dilemmas around us quickly and effectively.

Again the reality of the situation is such that I may in fact be earning more money than a missionary does. There may be no practical way of remedying the discrepancy. But the discrepancy has nothing to do with one of us living a more spiritual life than the other. It is an accident of war, a war we are both equally committed to. Whenever (in spite of very practical difficulties) there is a chance of evening up the discrepancy, all of us ought to be equally eager to do so.

Murder by Hair Spray   Some writers would at this point rise up to denounce the church in the West for luxuriating in wealth when Christians in other places are starving. And they would be right. We are callous and blind to the world's naked and hungry, be they our Christian brethren or our fellow human beings. While a devoted Christian lady is bothered because she cannot find her hair spray before setting out for her Sunday-school class, a Sudanese mother is watching her baby's eyes settle into the empty stare of death.

There are two sides to the question of course. It would be unjust to accuse the Sunday-school teacher of murder by hair spray. There are huge economic and logistical problems about the transfer of wealth and food from rich nations to starving ones. We need not feel condemned because we are surrounded by abundance. Rather we should praise and thank a bountiful God who pours unmerited blessings upon us.

On the other hand we have no right to brush the problem aside because of the complications. At the heart of the matter lies our dependence upon material things. We take them for granted. We accumulate them. We go into debt to acquire them, work longer hours to earn them. They enslave us. They enslave not only our bodies but our hearts which no longer have room for the crying of the needy, the starving and the dying.

Here lie the beginnings of our harlotry. We cherish our lovely buildings. We give payola to our pastors and missionaries so they will accept the spiritual responsibility that releases us to acquire things. We take our wealth for granted while in our hearts the groans of the starving and the screams of the tortured are muted into background muzak.

But our guilt does not stop here. We are part of a Christian world into which the worship of the golden cow has infiltrated more widely than most of us could ever dream. The church has become a harlot because her religion has become an industry. It is itself big business. And it is mandatory that we look carefully at the monster we have created.

7

RELIGION AS BUSINESS

Yesterday for the second time in ten minutes I bumped into Mitch on Kennedy Street. "Oh, Dr. White," he said as we passed, "the Bible society man said to ask you when his group could get to speak in your church. He said it's the only church in Manitoba they've never spoken in." Mitch is rejoicing in his newfound faith in Christ and is unaware at this point of a lot that goes on behind the scenes. I was nettled by the accusation (a false one), less by the Bible society itself (for which I have a profound respect) than by the never-ending pressure on some of us, a pressure that results from competitiveness among Christian institutions.

Why has the pressure arisen? Why do I groan at the pile of Christian junk mail on my desk and shrink from the task of going through it? Have I the right to use words like *Christian junk mail?* Most organizations tell me that while their own promotional literature is not junk, a great deal of what comes through the mail in Christ's name *is*. But where is the impartial judge of junk? What is it about the system that forces a Christian advertiser who fully recognizes my negative reaction to the pile of envelopes on my desk, to calculate how he can catch my eye and hold my attention by his own particular production? Why am I a target of so many advertising arrows, ducking and dodging from the archers who shoot them at me? And how can I tell which archers ought to be allowed to wound me most?

The Faith Principle   There is no simple answer to any of my questions. Nor, as I have already made it plain, is my aim to do a sociological treatise on evangelical fund raising. Rather it is to point once more to our reverence of the cow, which in part at least is behind the pressure. We trust in mass advertising more than we trust in God. We corrode the term *prayer support* to mean "financial support." And while we say we are trusting God to work *through* the means we are using to "acquaint the Christian public," we would feel rather frightened if the means were taken away. Poor old God would be left to stumble along without his crutches.

What we must do is to ask ourselves what we mean by faith in God. Do we really believe in the God of Moses, of Elijah and of Paul? And in asking the questions we need not lose ourselves in theological debate. We can look at the development of the "faith principle" in the modern missionary movement, its slow corruption and its eventual takeover by business philosophies and techniques within many Christian movements.

In the last century people like Hudson Taylor and George Müller grappled with some of the questions I have been raising and pioneered what is now referred to as the faith principle. Taylor took issue with a broad range of practices. He favored direction of missionary activity from the mission field itself rather than from the home base since local problems were less readily appreciated at home. Again, in a day when mission board members included distinguished clergy and members of the aristocracy, Taylor's board members were selected on the basis of their spiritual maturity rather than for their worldly prestige.

But his most exciting departure from the practice of his day had to do with raising funds. Boldly he enunciated the principle of "moving men's hearts through prayer to God alone," that is to say without appealing to people directly. God's work, he asserted, done in God's way would never lack God's supplies. Appeals for money were forbidden. Taylor refused to compete financially with other groups. Collections were not taken up at missionary meetings. Following one particular meeting a large sum of money from a private donor was politely refused. (The donor returned in the morning saying God had exercised his heart to give a much larger sum, which was accepted.)

The daring nature of the approach appealed to many people tired of Christian fund raising. True stories of dramatic instances of God's intervention awoke in the hearts of many Christians a hunger to deal more realistically with the living God. Steadily the method gained credence. As the China Inland Mission (founded by Taylor and now existing as the Overseas Missionary Fellowship) grew in size and prestige, a widening sector of evangelicals began to favor the same faith principle as a modus operandi for financing Christian work.

In retrospect it seems inevitable that the principle grew

not only to be widely accepted but adulterated and coated with hypocrisy. The words *by faith* eventually acquired a technical meaning and constituted a badge of spiritual respectability. Today we scarcely smile at the inconsistency of a Christian radio program closing with the words, "As you know this is a venture of faith. We are looking to God alone to meet *all* our needs, as you his people give generously to support this effort which reaches millions of needy people with the gospel. Our program costs $50,000 weekly. Please write and encourage us. Your letters mean much. ... We would like to send you at no charge a booklet entitled ..." and so on.

The inconsistency I refer to has nothing to do with asking for money. God's people need not be ashamed to request another's financial help. The inconsistency lies in the use of the words *by faith in God alone* when an overt advertising stratagem is being used.

In their day people like Taylor and Müller were doing something more important than enunciating a financial policy. They were re-evaluating their relationship with God. The question over which they grappled had to do with whether they were trusting in people, in methods or in God. It seemed to them that the only way they could be sure they were trusting in God only was to cut themselves off from what they would otherwise trust in. By all appearances God met them more than halfway. More important than the financial success of the policy was the joy they experienced in a new walk of faith.

Three Methods and a Fourth   Amy Carmichael once pointed out that Scripture supports three methods of raising funds: asking God's people for money, tent making (that is, earning your living to support your Christian service) and trusting God to supply by some means known in advance only to him. A fourth method is not scriptural: to profess to walk by faith in God alone and simultaneously to hint for funds or manipulate people into giving.

The three methods backed by Scripture are not mutually exclusive (Paul used all three) nor is any one method essentially superior to any other. We do not worship methods; we worship God. There is therefore nothing sacrosanct about the faith principle. I imagine all of us would agree that whatever method is used our faith should be in God rather than in the method. What distinguishes Hudson Taylor from the rest of us is that he was prepared to risk not only his own material security but that of a growing body of missionaries to a policy that was insanity—if God was not behind it. I gravely question that most of us have his kind of courage or faith, whatever we may profess about trusting God. At heart we have more confidence in the cow.

Nowadays we talk about *communication*. (We used to preach the gospel, whereas we now communicate the kerygma.) What is wrong, some people ask me, with communications?

I receive more communication than I know what to do with. I cannot possibly read, let alone "prayerfully consider" the mass of mimeographed letters, cards, announcements, photographs and magazines with which the mailman staggers to my door. A lonely widow bereft of friends may find comfort in this mountain of paper. For the five dollars she lovingly sends from her meager resources she may receive a heart-warming "personal letter" (little guessing it to be the synthetic product of an automatic typewriter) and even more prayer letters and magazines. Each day she goes eagerly to the mailbox feeling needed. She has become part of a whole much greater than herself. The ache of her loneliness is lessened, and for her the price is worth it. Soon she might offer her savings to the institution in an annuity. It would pay her an "income" in the form of interest on her death loan, but this interest is often less than what the institution would have to pay on a bank loan.

Do not misunderstand me. It is not the widow who is the loser but the organization. God loves a cheerful giver, so that a widow's mite dropped in the coffers of the modern Sadducees does not escape his attention. And I, for one, would have no wish to destroy the illusion that prompts her gift and that gives her solace.

What led to the increasing commercialization of so many Christian organizations? My next-door neighbor who recently became a Christian was bewildered at a missionary letter he received with a space at the bottom for him to indicate how much he might feel led to pledge.

"I didn't think real Christianity would be like this," he explained. "It's not that I don't want to give. But this is no different from the begging letter from the community club." Was he wrong in expecting Christianity to be different from the community club?

I admire my Christian business friends. I may not always agree with their views but I do not question their integrity. If the methods they urge upon Christian bodies arise from their business experience, who is to blame them? Yet how can we fail to see that so many fund-raising techniques are Christian only in the sense that Christians have adopted them? In every other sense they are identical with the techniques of modern business promotion.

Obviously I am leading into many serious and important

questions, the answers to which lie beyond the scope of this book. Advertising is not wrong. Persuasion is not wrong. Both become wrong either when the motive for using them is greed or when in using them we fail to treat human beings as human, ignore their dignity and view them as objects to manipulate. But the agonizing question business executives and Christian leaders face is, "At what point am I beginning to be guilty of these things?"

Taken singly, many of the techniques I have mentioned have something to commend them. It is only when we stand back to survey the scene as a whole that we begin to see what is happening. We have become so competent in our commercial competitiveness that God has been replaced on our boards of directors. His photograph, with a suitable brass plate, is still prominently and respectfully displayed in our head offices. (He is not dead. He has retired.) But if we are honest, most of us place the emphasis where our faith really lies—in modern methodology.

We must face the fact that the methods we use often undermine faith in God. This is what Christian leaders and business executives should beware of. There is a certain predictability about the results of mass advertising, provided it is properly carried out and its appeal correctly calculated. Mass advertising is an experimental science. It analyzes the results of this or that technique. It takes into account the moods and preoccupations of people both universally and in different geographical areas, and then exploits them. Are teen-agers uncertain of what others think of them? If so, perhaps they can be persuaded that their problem is bad breath or body odor and be induced to buy mouth washes or deodorants. Advertising is a skilled, highly complex device whereby people are not only informed about a product, but induced to purchase it whether they need it or not. Careful ongoing psychological and market studies continually update its methodology. Mass advertising pays off handsomely. It has revolutionized trade over the last one hundred years.

I do not wish to get involved at this point in a discussion on the complex sociological and ethical issues that mass advertising raises, but simply to note that many religious bodies have not been slow to make use of its techniques. They can be counted on even more than God can.

Advertising is not just persuasion. It also includes information. No one quarrels too much with information, provided it is *true* information. Tragically, Christian advertising does not always even inform accurately and sometimes depends on persuasion to an unhealthy degree.

A Christian organization that placed great stress on informing the Christian public of its activities adopted the following technique: A staff worker, following instructions from the head office, set herself a quota in personal soul winning. On achieving her goal of six or eight converts in a given month she would instruct each to write a brief account of his or her conversion. The account would be edited and the convert instructed to memorize it, so that he or she in turn could bear witness more readily and not be tongue-tied. A copy of the account would be included in the worker's next prayer letter along with a photograph of each convert.

In the above example I could look critically at several points, but for the moment I will hone in on one point: information. Obviously the technique has superb advertising potential. A monthly letter from which six or eight faces smile their tales of conversion at you will hit you with a wallop. As you read it you say to yourself, "Here God is indeed at work. This is something that merits my support."

Yet in the words of one worker, "The ink would scarcely be dry on the paper before most of the converts had ditched their 'faith.' This happened constantly."

The information in the prayer letters was misleading. Though there may have been no intent to deceive, the fact was that the faces that smiled when the photographs were taken were no longer smiling. The stories that appeared in the letter were not the stories being told when the letter was read.

What led to the unintentional deception? Was there in somebody's mind too great a need to "sell" the organization to the Christian public? Was the advancement of the organization a higher priority than the advancement of God's reputation? Did this lead to a lowering of the scriptural standards of truth? Was the whole thing just an elaborate sales pitch?

It did in fact reap superb financial returns which in the minds of many people meant that God was behind it. My own belief, however, is that we are viewing an example of the worship of the golden cow. And lest we hasten to reassure ourselves that our own methods are unimpeachable and that we would never countenance a scheme like the one I described, let me say that the details are irrelevant. What matters is what led to so great a need to sell a work to the Christian public. And here is something that involves us all.

The Pressures to Compete   Let me, for a few pages, adopt an ungodly perspective. I will try to put God in the back of my mind and view Christian work from a practical standpoint.

Christian organizations work in a competitive climate. While liquid gold is plentiful, there never seems to be enough of it flowing to maintain, much less to expand, all the existing organizations and churches, to say nothing of new ones. It follows that organizations compete for our dollars as well as for our prayers.

The fact is seldom discussed or even recognized. Mission leaders are aware of it because of the financial pressures they struggle under. Pastors are aware of it, especially pastors of "live" churches, because of the flow of mail across their desks. You would be surprised to know how many organizations might want their representative to speak, however briefly, on a given Sunday morning from certain church pulpits. One hears the phrase, "If we can get him in *there*," recur frequently during discussions about the strategy of deputation.

Certainly since World War 2 a kind of covert guerrilla warfare has been fought out among older and newer Christian organizations. While organizations often form alliances and friendships, when the fate of the individual organization is in question, it is every man for himself. Established denominations and some older interdenominational groups have money and prestige on their side. Solid downtown real estate, investments of other kinds plus complex annuity schemes give them a certain edge on the praying public's attention. Younger groups need to be (and often are) more aggressive to compete.

The war is the uglier because so few of us are willing to open our eyes to it. We pretend it does not exist. We have to, for we live with two irreconcilable ideas in our minds: the greatness of God and the facts of everyday life. So we gather together in certain associations, smiling our radiant smiles and giving warm Christian handshakes, all the time secretly assessing our brother's potential as a competitor. We do not really understand that God can easily supply all our needs. We forget that we should be as concerned with our brother's needs as with our own.

The weapons of our warfare are prayer letters, magazine articles, straightforward advertising, public speaking, films, tapes. On the whole we fight cleanly (at least in public). We devote our energies mainly to promoting our own causes and not to destroying other people's. However, in private many of us are expert character assassins. We have to be when we see money going in the wrong direction.

Some results of the competition are bizarre. We have already seen that the people who are least competent to judge how money should be spent are too often the ones who actually decide. The people who have money to give seem in practice to control the direction of Christian activity. It matters little whether such people are big givers or small givers; the rule holds.

If we are dealing with small givers, it is admittedly hard to say who exactly controls whom. (Remember, we are leaving God out of the picture for the moment.) Advertising tends to influence small givers more than large givers. It follows that the work that gets financial backing from small givers will be the work that is best put across (in film, by personal presentation or whatever) or which has the most psychological appeal. A scheme to airlift missionaries by helicopter to remote tribal regions will generally get more financial backing than a similar scheme to evangelize down river by canoe. In this example the outcome may be unimportant. You need less money for canoeing than for a helicopter. And as for effectiveness in evangelism, who can say which scheme is better? As one experienced tribal worker put it to me, "What a tremendous opportunity to spend four weeks in a canoe with a bunch of Indians. God really works in situations like that."

But there are other times when the outcome may matter more. What it boils down to is that the people who have the least knowledge and expertise in Christian work, and who may be the least discerning, give to whatever project seizes their imaginations most.

Big donors need to be cultivated with individual skill. Just as top sales representatives fly first class to negotiate with state legislators, so top Christian leaders negotiate with very wealthy Christians. Some of the latter are discerning and have neither the wish nor the desire to control the direction of Christian work. They take very seriously their responsibility as stewards. But some feel that their wealth itself entitles them to control. They reduce presidents of Bible schools to a state of panic and mission organizations to a crisis of faith by displaying their angry disagreement with one thing or another. Do they secretly relish their ability to cripple a work by withholding their support? Perhaps they see themselves holding, as it were, a majority of the shares in the Christian enterprise.

I am generalizing and oversimplifying very complex matters, but there is substance in my observations. What alarms most of us when we contemplate the scene differs very much, however, from what bothers God. It is perhaps time we brought him back into the discussion. We may grow alarmed at the thought that the control of Christian activity could sometimes lie in the hands of an immature Christian public and at other times in the hands of some opinionated Christian tycoon. It seems to us an unsatisfactory way of deciding what gets done and what doesn't. Possibly so. But we are thinking as the world thinks. We see money as more important than it really is. Money is powerless to generate spiritual activity and lack of money powerless to cramp it. We have forgotten to listen to God's plans and totally underestimated his power. We have assumed that misdirected money will thwart him. And so long as we think like this, we will be in danger of doing what so many Christian workers do: glorify God with our lips but bow down to the cow in practice.

Yet we must continue to look at the way Christian enterprise grows daily more indistinguishable from business enterprise. As we do so our focus must not be on success (whatever that means) but upon the devastating effects the transition has upon the church's relationship with God and with the honor of his name. For remember we are not concerning ourselves with the growth of the Christian industry but with the idolatry that underlies it.

Expansion and Blessing   Commerce thrives on two principles: expansion and competition. "You must never stand still," the proprietor of a small business will tell you. "Once you stop going forward, you start going backward." Do the words sound familiar? Did you perhaps think they were Christian principles? If they are, they were first borrowed from business.

It is natural to want to expand an enterprise. Growth symbolizes success. All too readily the small Christian organization, delighted to have brought the gospel to a thousand people, begins to assume that it must strengthen its stakes and lengthen its cords. But expansion can take place at the expense of quality. And expansion can intoxicate us with the scene of glory ahead. David paid a terrible price for his egocentric head count of Israel (1 Chron. 21). And somewhere along the line so many Christian evangelists and churches have done the same. Nobody could tell you when or how it happened, but little by little the church becomes important in and of itself. It used to pray for revival because it longed to honor God. Now it prays for revival because attendance improves when there is revival. Spiritual principles become of importance primarily in that they foster expansion.

And the moment you set your sights on expansion, inevitably you find yourself competing. Some Christians see nothing wrong with this. One prominent Christian leader unabashedly told me that when he had been in business he had found that it was best to start a new business in the places where business was already thriving. In a similar way he felt he should start a new Christian group "where the competition is best," that is, where other groups were already working.

Paul's principles were different. He refused to build on another's foundation, preaching where Christ had not previously been named. Yet again and again missionaries and Christian workers find themselves involved in competition rather than cooperation.

As a relatively green missionary trying to help Latin American students, I learned all too soon what Christian competition meant. One day in Lima, Peru, I found myself praying and planning with a Christian Mexican student. He had received much help from me when I was associated with the International Fellowship of Evangelical Students and now he felt that call of God to evangelize Mexican universities. His Mexican colleagues and I suggested he complete his degree (a few months away) before devoting all his time to student evangelism. We also discussed and my student friend stressed the importance of the venture being truly Mexican—with a Mexican board and, if possible, Mexican financing. Until the student finished his degree he had agreed to act as an agent in Mexico for a Christian student magazine published in Argentina.

The next day my friend told me he had received a message to make a collect call from Lima to a number in the United States where a prominent Christian leader, also engaged in student evangelism, wished to speak with him. I waited outside the phone booth as he made the call.

"He wants me to fly up to the States to talk with him," he told me as he emerged.

"Will you go?" I asked.

"He will pay my passage both ways."

"When will you go?"

"As soon as I get my tickets."

I felt bewildered.

"What does he want?"

"He says he wants to help students in Mexico."

"Did you tell him what you were doing?"

"Yes. He said, 'Have those people got you to sign anything?' He asked me twice, 'Are you sure you've signed no papers?' So I told him no, that I hadn't signed anything."

I was shocked. Was the implication that only signed commitments mattered?

He looked at me, hoping I would understand. "I want to do what is best for Mexico."

"Of course, and if you feel God wants you to go, you must go."

"Well, I'm not sure. But perhaps I should go and see what

111

he has to say. He wants me to get to know their work and then see how I feel."

I was too naive to believe what my mind told me was happening. I thought that nobody who was a Christian would use money (in the shoestring operation I was engaged in, telephone calls to the States or sudden trips there were unheard of) to contact a novice already engaged in one operation and try to capture him for another. Nowadays I would have no hesitation in squaring with such a student so that at least he could see the issues straight. As it was he went as a lamb, and as a lamb was led into a new fold.

Maybe God meant it that way. But I know God didn't approve of the way it was done. I cite the instance as a flagrant example of what is happening in Christian work constantly though usually in a less flagrant manner.

If your response is one of incredulity or indignation, you fail to understand what is happening. Expansion is unthinkingly accepted among Western Christians as something good and desirable in itself. And by expansion I do not mean the spread of the gospel, but the growth of particular institutions. Expanding organizations come into conflict over money, territory and workers. At times mature thinking prevails, and there is cooperation and collaboration. But equally often, conflict results in the kind of competitiveness I have already described, which is not the less fierce for being described in pious clichés as "a matter for prayer."

So the operation gets bigger. If smaller groups get crowded out, maybe that proves that God has lost interest in them. They should have had more "faith." Just as in laissez faire capitalism so in the Christianizing industry, the law of the survival of the fittest must be the law of God himself.

As new organizations come into being, the finances of older groups are threatened. It may be that a denominational missionary society finds funds are flowing to an upstart interdenominational society. Or again, a well-established interdenominational society discovers that its constituency is now more interested in newer groups.

Obviously some Christian groups feel the pinch more than others. Some denominational missions have large reserves of capital. Wherever the pinch is felt most keenly, there the battle rages most fiercely. And a battle it is. Behind the firm handshakes and ecclesiastical jocularity, a struggle for economic survival often rages, nonetheless deadly for being covert.

No one really knows what the financial potential of Christianity is. Like a great cow the Christian public itself chews contentedly as scores of hands grab greedily for her udders. She is not likely to dry up for the meadows in which she grazes are lush with green dollars. But the milkers grow anxious.

Why is it that several Christian organizations (and many more for all I know) have placed their public relations in the hands of a "Christian public relations" firm? How can it be possible that an outstanding Christian leader will allow his prayer letters (and some of the rest of his public correspondence) to be submitted to a public relations expert to be vetted before it goes out?

Once again it is often a matter of support. A Christian organization feels it has to project the kind of image that will not offend those who have given for years and that at the same time will "awaken prayer interest" in a wider constituency. And image projecting calls for professional skills. One Christian leader spoke to me of the "pretty fancy footwork" needed to keep diverse supporting groups happy. A wrong sentence may cost several thousand dollars. The more I study Christian organizations, the harder it becomes to distinguish them (in their policies and methods of working) from commercial enterprises.

The examples I have been giving are only a few, but they form part of a picture which convinces me that we revere the cow more than we believe in Yahweh. Not all organizations are so bitten by the success bug as some I have described. Nevertheless most have in some degree succumbed to commercialized methods of fund raising.

Most send carefully worded begging letters plus postage-guaranteed envelopes. Others pursue different sources of potential income. Is someone making a will? Then explain how tax laws will make the legacy to a Christian group worth twice as much. Does a widow need security yet want to give to Christian work? An annuity scheme may be just the answer: cash for the Bible school, income for the widow. Is there a death in the family? Then why not ask friends to give to a Christian cause rather than give flowers? Who can argue against the logic of money "wasted on" flowers when Bibles are at stake? (Who could argue against money wasted on perfume poured over Christ's feet when the poor were going hungry?) So Christian organizations, like dignified vultures, join the funeral directors, the flower sellers, the needy relatives in a stately dance for pickings around the contents of a satin-lined casket.

I do not know whether to be amused or saddened by the double messages Christian groups send out. The first message is: God is with us in a big way. Climb on board while you have the chance! The second message is: Something dreadful is happening. We're about to be shipwrecked on the shoals of financial need. To get both messages across at the same time calls for verbal dexterity.

According to the begging mail my wife leaves on my desk, the church is in dire straits. God is apparently doing a terrific job through all the Christian organizations that write me, but he has run into a financial crisis that threatens to undo everything. In the nick of time he was saved last year because he himself prompted people to give. This year it looks as though he might not be able to make ends meet. So we must trust God and rescue him at the same time.

A Conference on Filthy Lucre?   How can we stop the tide? We live in the age of conventions. We congregate in large numbers to hear big-name speakers speak to important issues. Who will organize a convention where Christian leaders from all over the world meet to discuss the place of money in God's work, to discuss faith and the ethics of fund raising? The problem is so widespread and so complex that I feel helpless when I ask myself what the solution is.

I would like to see greater minds than mine, leaders of experience and seniority gather in Lausanne or any other suitable place to talk about filthy lucre. There might be fireworks, but there might also be fruit. Is it impossible that God should revive his people as far down as their pocketbooks? Is it impossible for the Holy Spirit to show us how we may reform our principles and practices? For only if we gather together and face the issue squarely, will anything be done.

Some experienced Christian leaders have already made their views known. In December 1977 *Eternity* magazine published an interview with Edward Hales, Director of Field Services for the National Association of Evangelicals.

Several vital issues were touched on in the report.

First in importance (to my mind) was the tension between the teaching of stewardship and techniques for fund raising. Christian leaders have a duty to teach God's people both the responsibility and the joys of giving. Such teaching has a spiritual goal. Its aim is not to raise money but to set Christians free from their bondage to money, to teach them the liberty of liberality and thus to increase their joy in the Lord.

Techniques for fund raising have, on the other hand, a material aim. They do not ask, "How can I help the Christian public find freedom?" They ask, "How can I induce the Christian public to cough up?" The second question may have some validity, but it is of less consequence than the first. Christian leaders both in churches and in parachurch organizations must ask themselves, "Which concerns me more, economic survival for our work or spiritual freedom for God's people?" Tension exists between the two goals. It is impossible to be equally concerned with both, and one must take priority over the other.

A second point arises from the first. A church pastor is in a position to feel the pull of both goals. Both the church's economic viability and the spiritual needs of its members concern him. He is therefore asking a real question when he asks whether he should be dominated with economic or spiritual concerns. If he is wise and godly, he will choose to teach not only a sense of financial responsibility to his flock but how they may find release from mammon. He should not cease to be concerned about economic questions, but his prime goal will be pastoral.

The position is very different in what have been described as parachurch organizations (such as interdenominational bodies). Leaders of such groups have a split constituency. They are responsible on the one hand for the spiritual well-being of people who have become Christians because of their endeavors. They are also responsible to the Christian public to whom they look for funding. It becomes much easier under such circumstances to have spiritual concern for the first constituency while viewing the second merely as a source of income. For the pastor, no such split exists. When he surveys the congregation, he surveys both the source of the church's income and the flock to whom he ministers.

Parachurch organizations are thus exposed more than churches to the temptations of stressing fund-raising techniques rather than being primarily concerned with the spiritual liberty of the givers. It is in fact very difficult for them to have a deep and godly concern for the Christian public.

Some might ask, "Should we not then question the validity of parachurch structures?" The question is huge and has been ably dealt with elsewhere. I would propose an alternative and more down-to-earth question. How may we, the Christian public, protect parachurch organizations from becoming milkmaids of the golden cow?

Hales, in the *Eternity* interview, pointed out that in the United States the federal government has already become concerned and that legislation to control dishonest practices seems inevitable sooner or later. It will indeed be a sad day when government action replaces self-regulation on the part of God's people. But in the meantime some form of self-regulation could start among us.

Hales also points to three reports on the ethics of fund raising, reports from the American Association of Fund-Raising Council, the National Catholic Development Council and the Christian Stewardship Council. All of these have valuable suggestions. Christian leaders in parachurch organizations as well as in denominational mission organizations would do well to study the reports.

On the other hand the Christian public must become more sophisticated. Christians must learn to insist on adequate financial reports from bodies to whom they give money. They must learn how to evaluate such financial reports and be aware that some reports conceal the amount of money spent on things like promotion. They must ask, "Exactly how much cash did the organization have in hand at the year end? How much money is spent *on doing the job* and how much on overhead?" An organization that spends fifty per cent of its income on keeping itself going should be scrutinized with care.

More important still we must become more discerning about the goals of each organization and whether they are being fulfilled. How honest are the reports of work carried out? Is the organization doing what it says it is doing? We cannot guarantee that we will never be conned, and it really does not matter if we sometimes are. But at least we will be trying by an increase in what Hales calls "donorism" (seeking to protect the donor as consumerism seeks to protect the consumer) to provide some incentive for better financial practices among Christian organizations.

Of course, I could be less ambitious than suggesting an international conference. If you are a leader, why do you not convene a retreat in your Christian organization to hash such matters over? The subject is dangerous, I know. It would be better still if various Christian organizations could sign some sort of armistice or treaty to de-escalate the fund-raising race in a manner that would not upset the balance of power too much. But what is to stop a unilateral de-escalation of fund raising? Would it be too risky? Do you fear that the finger of God might write, "MENE, MENE, TEKEL and PARSIN" over your organization? Then face your fear. Face it together before God.

I do not believe that the extension of God's kingdom is held up by lack of money. Yes, indeed, Christian organizations (both denominational and interdenominational) are under financial stress. Of course their workers live sacrificially, doing without many things the rest of us have. But the financial problem is spiritually peripheral. I believe underpaid Christian workers are as much the victims of Christian empire building and of wrong ways of going about things as they are of callous indifference on our part. We have become slaves of Christian institutions rather than servants of Christ. And our institutions in turn are harlots painting their lips with scarlet to appeal to a golden cow.

But there is worse to follow. For the cow is not content that we worship her, especially if our worship is only half-conscious worship. She wishes to reduce our God to someone who can be bought and sold at bargain rates in a dime store, and his people to laboratory rats who can be programmed to become nothing more than mechanical followers of Jesus.

8

DESENSITIZED TO DESECRATION

Josephus in his *Antiquities of the Jews* (XX, VI, 3) describes how Cumanus, fearing a tumult in the Temple during the Passover at Jerusalem, posted armed soldiers in the cloisters. On the fourth day one of the soldiers, perhaps inflamed by wine, "let down his breeches and did expose his privy members to the multitude, which put those that saw him into a furious rage, and made them cry out that this impious action was not done to reproach them but God himself." On the surface, Jewish indignation seemed to be directed against a foul desecration of the sacred precincts and of the God who presenced himself there.

The incident is one of several desecrations of the Temple that ancient manuscripts record. Antiochus Epiphanes erected an idol in the holy place. Years later, a Roman army set fire to the Temple, defying Titus who himself appears to have been distraught over the desecration (Josephus, *Wars of the Jews,* VI, II, iv).

Jews were understandably appalled, reacting violently. And we can see at once that obscene gestures, looting, burning and the erection of idols in a place where the holy Creator condescended to dwell between the cherubs constitutes an abomination.

Yet when at the beginning of this book we looked together at the startling sight of a violent Jesus lashing the Temple precincts free of commerce, the offense which he protested—if it can be called an offense—seems at first not to compare in gravity with the foul desecrations carried out by pagans. In what then lies the offensiveness of desecration? And why should commerce in the Temple precincts evoke an outburst of divine rage when obscenity and idolatry seem to have passed unnoticed?

We may perhaps excuse the pagans on two counts. For one thing they may never have had an opportunity to learn reverence for Yahweh. And for another, the desecrators seem not to have been thinking about Yahweh so much as aiming a calculated insult at Jewish national pride. When one man calls another "a son of a bitch," he never thinks of the mother he maligns but of the man he wishes to enrage.

And if we look carefully at the Jewish responses to the desecrations, we discover that the insults had found their mark. Jewish anger was not over God's honor but over their own. Pagans and Jews each dragged Yahweh into the argument as a means of getting at the other. For instance the Jews accused Cumanus of having incited the ribald soldier to perpetrate his obscenity. It is clear from Josephus's description of the scene that they were out to make political capital out of the incident. Their "religious" indignation was a sort of political blackmail bereft of any real concern for Yahweh.

The pagans had never learned reverence for him. The Jews had forgotten what reverence meant, had forgotten the lessons of the burning bush, of the flaming mountain that could not be touched and of the earth that opened to swallow the sons of Korah. They had been desensitized, as we ourselves have been, to desecration.

Unmelted Snow, Framed by Brown Earth   In one form or another the thing I am calling desensitization is common enough. While he never uses the word, C. S. Lewis in his book, *The Abolition of Man,* charges some modern educators with desensitizing children to things in life which ought to awaken respect, awe and reverence. Lewis sides with the ancient philosophers in asserting that the most valuable function of education is to inculcate in the young what he calls *ordinate* (appropriate) responses to creation, to the words and actions of people around them, to good and evil—indeed to every aspect of life.

"Until quite modern times," he writes, "all teachers and even all men believed the universe to be such that certain emotional reactions on our part could be either congruous or incongruous to it—believed, in fact, that objects could *merit* our approval or disapproval, our reverence, or our contempt" (C. S. Lewis, *The Abolition of Man,* p. 25). He quotes Plato who describes the well-nurtured youth as one "who would see most clearly whatever was amiss in ill-made works of man or ill-grown works of nature, and with a just distaste would blame and hate the ugly even from his earliest years and would give delighted praise to beauty, receiving it into his soul and being nourished by it, so that he becomes a man of gentle heart. All this before he is of an age to reason; so that when reason at length comes to him, then, bred as he has been, he will hold out his hands in welcome and recognize her because of the affinity he bears to her" (Plato, *The Republic,* 402A). A thousand years later St. Augustine was to describe virtue as *ordo amoris,* "such a regulation of my affections that I shall render to every object an appropriate kind and degree of love, or hatred" (Augustine, *De Civ. Dei,* XV22).

I remember walking with two friends across the English moors in springtime. Pushing through bog and bracken, we were suddenly surprised by a cluster of pine trees where the last of the snow lay unmelted, framed by brown earth and deep green clusters of needles, washed by golden light from a late afternoon sun. Two of us stopped.

"Oh!" I said, catching my breath. "Isn't that incredible!"

"Beautiful," my friend breathed, awe in his voice. "Just beautiful."

The third member of the party hesitated, staring with a puzzled expression first in the direction we were looking and then at both of us. "What is it? What are you looking at?"

"Don't you see?"

"Only some trees and snow. It's very nice, but...."

Some people would say, disagreeing with Lewis, that no beauty existed and that our responses reflected nothing more than differences in our subjective feelings. To this I would make two observations. First, I am grateful for the response I experienced to the sight of the snow and the pines. I am richer and happier for that response, and I do not want to change places with my second friend whom I saw as blind to the beauty. My second point brings us nearer to our subject. All Christians, whether we agree with Plato, Aristotle, Augustine and Lewis about ordinate affections or not, must agree that an encounter with God *should* awaken in us awe, reverence, worship and adoration. There is an ordinate response to God, and he who lacks it, who is desensitized to glory, and in whom wonder and fear are no longer awakened, is greatly to be pitied. Such Christians remind me of an appalling encounter some of my colleagues and I had with a schizophrenic patient.

She was admitted to the hospital after finding her parents dead in bed as a result of a double suicide. "Oh, dear! What did you do?" one of my colleagues asked her.

"I called the dentist."

"The dentist?"

"To cancel their appointments. They couldn't keep dental appointments if they were dead." The reply came with no emotion, in a quiet sing-song voice.

However we may explain the woman's response, we recognize that it was not *ordinate to* the situation. Most of us would have responded to a similar situation with shock, horror, profound dismay and grief. Not to respond in this way would indicate that something had gone profoundly wrong with us, as it had in fact in the patient I referred to. I listened, appalled and frightened, by the hollow echo of a personality that seemed to be living in the woman's body.

We can see by now that it is impossible to separate desensitization to desecration from desensitization to divinity. He who does not tremble before the radiance of glory will be tone deaf to desecration. We must first be awakened to beauty before we are horrified by Philistinism.

The Source of Reverence   I know of no more moving

125

description of what I am calling an ordinate response to deity than the one found in Kenneth Grahame's children's story, *The Wind in the Willows*. Mole and rat have been searching all night for Portly, a lost baby otter whose parents are stricken with grief because they fear him drowned. At dawn the two animals encounter him on an island above a weir in the river. He lies sleeping between the sheltering hooves of the god Pan. I quote the section in full, not as a tribute to a heathen god, for Grahame had no such purpose in the passage. Rather he was revealing in the allegory his own experience of reverence for God, and doing so with such exquisite sensitivity and insight that the passage remains a model of the ordinate response I am discussing.

"This is the place of my song-dream, the place the music played to me," whispered the Rat, as if in a trance. "Here, in this holy place, here if anywhere, surely we shall find Him!"

Then suddenly the Mole felt a great Awe fall upon him, an awe that turned his muscles to water, bowed his head, and rooted his feet to the ground. It was no panic terror—indeed he felt wonderfully at peace and happy— but it was an awe that smote and held him and, without seeing, he knew it could only mean that some august Presence was very, very near. With difficulty he turned to look for his friend, and saw him at his side cowed, stricken, and trembling violently. And still there was utter silence in the populous bird-haunted branches around them; and still the light grew and grew.

Perhaps he would never have dared to raise his eyes, but that, though the piping was now hushed, the call and the summons still seemed dominant and imperious. He might not refuse, were Death himself waiting to strike him instantly, once he had looked with mortal eye on things rightly kept hidden. Trembling, he obeyed, and raised his humble head; and then, in that utter clearness of the imminent dawn, while Nature, flushed with incredible color, seemed to hold her breath for the event, he looked in the very eyes of the Friend and Helper; saw the backward sweep of the curved horns gleaming in the growing daylight; saw the stern, hooked nose between the kindly eyes that were looking down on them humorously, while the bearded mouth broke into a half-smile at the corners; saw the rippling muscles on the arm that lay across the broad chest, the long supple hand still holding the pan-pipes only just fallen away from the parted lips; saw the splendid curves of the shaggy limbs disposed in majestic ease on the sward; saw, last of all, nestling between his very hooves, sleeping soundly in entire peace and contentment, the little, round, podgy, childish form of the baby otter. All this he saw, for one moment breathless and intense, vivid on the morning sky; and still, as he looked, he lived; and still, as he lived, he wondered.

"Rat!" he found breath to whisper, shaking. "Are you afraid?"

"Afraid?" murmured the Rat, his eyes shining with unutterable love. "Afraid! Of *Him*? Oh, never, never! And yet—and yet—Oh, Mole, I am afraid!"

Then the two animals, crouching to the earth, bowed their heads and did worship. (K. Grahame, *The Wind in the Willows*, pp. 117-18)

Anyone who has experienced the immediacy of God's presence will recognize at once the authenticity with which Grahame writes. And anyone who has experienced what Grahame describes carries in his bosom the embers of a precious fire, praying those embers will never, never be put out, valuing more than all earth's treasures a memory and the awakened capacity to adore.

Some of the offenders in the Temple may never have known such a capacity. Others had been desensitized to it by greed, by cruelty, by callous indifference to God's people, by self-righteousness, by arrogance and by contempt.

Temple officials and Sadducees had been desensitized. Something was profoundly wrong with them. Was this what aroused the wrath of the Lamb? I am inclined to doubt it. Their fate, that is to say their terrible insensitivity to sacred things, might awaken horror and dismay. But surely it calls for pity, rather than for rage.

But the evil their desensitization led to was greater than their personal loss of ordinate worship. There actions were no less than blasphemous. While angels and demons looked on they defiled the only holy place on earth.

God has, of course, no *need* for our reverence. He does not feed on our awe and adoration. But he who is worthy that all creation bow before him crying, "Holy, holy, holy is the Lord of hosts! All time and space are full of his glory!" knows that unless men are moved to utter such words from the bottom of their hearts, they will neither know what it is to be created human nor what joy and glory are all about. And he longs that we be liberated to know the full purpose of our creation, to know him and to enjoy him forever.

When Jesus shipped the irreligious garbage from Temple precincts, it was the hub of a system of worship which alone could claim to show people a way to the knowledge of the Holy. It was a place where human beings might experience an encounter with their maker.

While the loving heart of Yahweh drew people to himself, the Sadducees were hiding him from view. Those who should have known better, whose position and whose training should have made them windows and doors through whom people saw the God of heaven, had become sponsors of cheap buys on pigeons. They had exploited the yearnings of the humble and meek, turning them into a means of gain.

T-shirts, Pencils, Bumper Stickers   Up to now we have been looking at some fairly straightforward forms of the exploitation of the Christian public. The Bible school that bilks old ladies of their savings is at least doing so for what it sees as a good cause. Annuity schemes may be a form of spiritual harlotry, but they do not constitute a *racket,* at least not in the popularly used sense of the term. The Bible-school staff does not commonly line its pockets with the widow's savings.

The Jesus-pencil-bumper-sticker thing belongs to a different order of spiritual obscenity. It is desecration of a fouler kind. It has to do with the greed that fills one's wallet from the fears, the joys and the tenderness that bring God and man together. It is desecration.

But at once I hit difficulties. There are any number of ways of defending a sweat shirt from which "I love Jesus" blooms from an adolescent girl. Are sweat shirts not needed? Is it wrong to sell them? Is it wrong to make a profit on the sale of clothing? And whatever could be wrong with encouraging a teen-age girl to advertise the fact that she loves Jesus?

But I ask, Who made the shirt? Was he concerned with making an honest profit on the manufacture and sale of the garment? How did he himself feel about the blessed name of Jesus? Was he really trying to combine an honest living with a chance to honor the name of Christ, or was he an opportunist, seizing the chance of making a few more bucks by exploiting a cheap and silly fad? If he was doing the latter, he was guilty of desecration, and we who buy or tolerate such T-shirts are party to his desecration.

We humans get desensitized quickly to things which horrify us. It happened to me with human bodies when I was a medical student. One day I stood for the very first time with a knife in my hand beside a naked corpse on a marble slab. My first dissection. Opposite me stood a Christian girl, also a medical student. We both took very deep breaths in spite of the slight odor, and our eyes were wide and staring. I touched the cold skin covering the body and drew back my hand, gripping my scalpel more firmly. I looked at my partner's frightened brown eyes.

"D'you want to have a go first?" I asked unchivalrously.

"No, you first," she breathed.

Yet within two weeks it was all old hat. We could even (and sometimes did) joke about matters which would make other people's hair stand on end.

One can get used to almost anything. And we Christians are so desensitized to desecration that we do not notice it even though it surrounds us.

A Religion without Reverence   Admittedly many desecrations are spawned by people who could not care less about the things of God. The boom in gospel music is largely exploitation of a popular mood by pagan businessmen. We cannot blame Christians for what pagan merchants do.

Again making money out of religion is not in itself desecration. Servants of the gospel have to live by the gospel.

Therefore profits on Christian literature, tapes, records, preaching does not constitute a desecration of sacred things. Rather it is when greed sees the chance of a quick profit from those whose hearts have been made vulnerable by their yearning for God that desecration's ugly fungus is spawned.

I remember seeing once the transfigured face of a girl in an evangelistic meeting. She was kneeling and had suddenly looked up, her cheeks awash with tears. It must have been in that moment that the wonder of God's love had broken over her, for the expression of joy that shone blindingly from her was indescribable. For a moment I stared, fascinated. Then instinctively I turned away and bowed my head.

But supposing I had felt like capturing and exploiting commercially what I saw? Supposing I could have filmed that moment with the kind of magic that can transcribe emotion and use it to advertise an evangelistic technique I was perfecting, so that I would be asked to preach more widely? Or just to make money? I never do so, of course, yet the same sort of thing is so much a part of the current religious scene that we do no more than shrug.

Why get upset about an "I love Jesus" sweat shirt? The Chinese never used to pronounce the word for God. It was too sacred. The word for heaven would take its place. The ancient Hebrews had similar feelings about the name Yahweh (Jehovah). As a Christian I feel perfect liberty to pronounce the name Jesus. But if I pause to think when I pronounce it, it has a powerful effect on me. I am reminded of a Creator who did not despise a woman's uterus, who allowed himself to be reduced to an infant so that he could fully share my humanity, who associated though he was

God with poor peasants, who despised the horrors of death and sin, vanquished death itself and rose again. I know that one day at this same name of Jesus every knee shall bow. Can you ask me then how I feel when that same name is used as a gimmick to sell sweat shirts? (And if you are naive enough to feel that the gimmick can be a "witness," you should learn the difference between advertising and witness.)

You might argue that I have chosen something very trivial that should be ignored. For a long time I would have agreed with you. Yet as I see the rage that the Son of God expressed against the moneychangers, I know that the issue can never be a trivial one.

North American Christianity is religion without reverence. Other religious traditions have at least expressed contempt and disgust at the sellers of idols, at religious post cards, medals and other cheap junk. But where are the voices of protest here? The Lamb of God is reduced to bright pink on a bumper sticker.

The same desecration may take many subtle forms, and Christians can be drawn into collusion with the moneymakers. How, for instance, should we view Christian tours to the Holy Land? Pastors are involved as subagents of travel agencies. The pastor gets a free trip as a tour guide. Before long he may be making tours regularly and may even take his wife along. The travel company benefits by the increased turnover of sales resulting from the pastor's Christian contacts. The pastor gets a change (by no means a restful one) in his routine.

Once again the question may be asked, What harm is there in all this? We could go further. Are we not doing a great good by gratifying the longing of many Christian people? Will they not see the very places where our Savior's feet have trodden? What an opportunity we are giving them!

What an opportunity.... Do the words sound familiar? They appear too frequently in promotional literature. Are we not in fact doing what some Roman Catholics have done around their shrines and cathedrals (and what other Roman Catholics have detested) all down the ages, and merely desecrated the sense of the holy by commercial opportunism? We have not sinned against the people who take the tours. We have certainly not sinned against the stones of Jerusalem, though we may have contributed to a semiworship of them. Most of the tourists return with glowing eyes and burning hearts. We sin against God by exploiting the financial potential of those very glowing hearts. For the question has to be asked, Where does the interest of the tour promoters lie? In the glory of Jesus? In the happiness of his people? Or in the turnover of the ticket sales? A house of prayer can so quickly become a den of thieves.

A Profit-Spotting Spirit Commercial desecration, then, cannot be defined in terms of any specific form of religious commercial enterprise. It has to do with the spirit that too readily spots the profit potential in the longings of God's children. The heart is deceitful above all things and desperately wicked. Of the Christian publisher I ask, Which is uppermost in your mind, the needs of the church or a potential best seller? I know we have to be practical. I know best sellers can supplement the loss on some poorly selling book that has a needed ministry, but it is not of these things I speak. Rather it is of the eye that spots a book which will pander to the credulity of the spiritually naive, that will cash in on the latest spiritual fad, that will be part of a boom. More than this I ask, Is your heart cold and cynical? Are you in it for the profit or for your company's growth potential?

And the same questions could be asked of organizers of Christian conferences and holiday centers, of bookstores, tape ministries, Christian real-estate developers, pastors of growing churches. I cannot answer the questions myself. I only have a strong sense as I survey the whole religious scene (in North America particularly) that if Jesus were to come among us again, he would still find moneychangers in the Temple precincts and react as violently now as he did then.

What can we all do about it?

Well, the local bookstores would not suffer terribly if we boycotted stupid items like "Honk if you love Jesus" bumper stickers, Jesus sweat shirts, Jesus pencils, bookmarks, praying hands, charismatic jewelry and such sacrilegious garbage. Why don't pastors call on their congregations for such a boycott? How about adult Sunday-school class discussions on "Modern Moneychangers and How to Overturn Their Tables"? How about a discussion on "Commerce and Tours to the Holy Land"?

The problem is that sacrilege cannot be defined. It arises both from spiritual colorblindness and from callous indifference to the longings of those whose hearts seek after God. We therefore must examine our own hearts. We can ask ourselves whether we have been lured into the seats of the moneychangers. We can ask God to show us the motives in our hearts in any matter where money has to do with the sacred person of our Lord and God. If the Holy Spirit shows us we are in any way involved in desecration, we can quit. There may be financial loss. There may be embarrassment. But there will be refreshment and renewal in our lives. We are not ourselves called to plait a whip of cords. Our rage is not called for, only our repentance. Where we see, or where we *think* we see desecration flourishing, we should pray both "Spirit, convict" and "Father, forgive!" Apart from this we must confine ourselves to not touching the unclean thing ourselves.

It has its roots in the worship of the golden cow, and we must smash her altars from our own hearts, our households and our businesses. Her worship dishonors the name of our God. And as we shall see in the next chapter it strips the divine likeness from the face of his creature—man, male and female.

9

THE HUMAN MACHINE

We commit our whoredoms not only with the god of greed and with the golden cow. We also worship the great god science and bow before his laboratory-coated priests. We have more respect for archaeology, psychology, psychiatry, sociology than we have for the Scriptures. Do we not rush to say, "The Bible must be true *because science has proved it*"? But what are we saying? We are saying that science is the ultimate authority.

Why are we so anxious for science to confirm the Scriptures? Is it not because we have more confidence in the "assured findings of modern science" than in the Word of God so that we feel ill at ease with the latter until the former has come to its rescue?

And nowhere does our worship of science prove more disastrous than when we pay heed to its view of the human race. Let us pause to look at the confusion our idolatry has wrought in our attitude to our fellow men and women.

Matter Is All That Matters   In chapter four I contrasted the doctrinaire materialism of communism with what I called pragmatic materialism in the West. Doctrinaire materialism asserts that only matter (or energy which is another form of matter) exists. We live in a universe which has nothing "outside" it, which has always existed. Randomly moving particles cause other particles to move. The universe, if not a gigantic machine (lacking the precision and uniformity of machines) is yet related by complex chains of cause and effect, and what appear to be laws.

Part of the system is humanity itself. It is important to grasp this. Humans are not the controllers of or even observers of the system, but an integral part of it. Materialism, taken to its logical conclusions, asserts that we cannot make decisions (though we all *think* we do). We are programmed like computers. If our behavior seems complex, it is merely because of the complexity and sophistication of our programs.

Such a concept of humanity is full of problems, a discussion of which lies beyond my present purpose. All I wish to emphasize now is that to the materialist, people are not capable of logical "thought" or "decision." We have no will of our own. If we knew the details of the programs, we could predict every word and action. We are robots. Our emotions can be turned on at the touch of psychological buttons. With sufficient understanding we could (and can) be made to laugh or cry like a Mattel doll.

Pragmatic materialism on the other hand does not teach that matter is all that exists but that matter is all that *matters*.

Our actions and attitudes are valuable if they contribute to producing and accumulating things. Many governments are pragmatically materialistic. When they say, "The greatest good for the greatest number of people," they are thinking of cars, homes, jobs, clothes, medical care and so on. Most middle-aged parents think this way too.

But notice. On the surface it looks as though we who admit to being pragmatically materialist at least honor human dignity and worth. Yet closer examination shows that this is not the case.

The catchwords of pragmatic materialism are, "Get a good education and you'll get ahead," "Money talks," "Money isn't everything but it can make life a whole lot easier." Materialism sees national well-being hitched to the rising star of the Gross National Product.

You may say, "At least we are concerned with human well-being." But we are talking about human dignity, not human well-being. How, for instance, do we go about "improving the well-being of people?" We do so at the expense of their dignity. We subject them to media manipulation so they will buy what we want them to buy, wear what we want them to wear, eat what we want them to eat. Whatever we may profess about believing in human dignity, our actions betray us. We base our commercials on theories that assume people are either laboratory rats or computers. We then proceed to strip them of dignity in order to load them with things.

I have suggested that many Christian groups contradict their profession of valuing spiritual things more than physical. Their approach both to life and to their ministry is commercial. Christians who pride themselves in possessing life eternal often appear to live by the rule: Seek ye first the kingdom of the cow with careful budgeting, and many fringe benefits will be added unto you. Our actions and our beliefs do not jibe. In the same way, some who say they see people as machines (for example, communists in countries where they are not in power) treat them as though they were made in the image of God while we who teach that they have an eternal destiny treat them as though they were machines.

Let me be specific. Take the example of Christian begging letters. I have already indicated that experience has taught experts how to open one's billfold. People are more likely to give if you enclose a prepaid envelope and a blank check. The letter (or booklet or folder) must arrest their attention. It must be easy to read. It must make them see how much you appreciate their interest, how important their contributions will be. In a word it must psych them into giving. You adapt your method of begging to human responses. The "angle" you work on in your advertising is the one most likely to produce the response you are after.

Commercial enterprises describe the method openly and unashamedly; Christians squirm uncomfortably or else indignantly justify their begging techniques. "How can you call it begging when what we are doing is encouraging people to experience the blessing of giving to God?" My answer remains, Which concerns you more, the blessings for the people who get your begging letter or their responses in your return mail? In using commercial gimmicks to raise money, you are treating Christians the same way behavioral psychologists treat trained rats.

Evangelistic Manipulation By worshiping the great god science you not only show your lack of confidence in God but also your contempt for humanity. The moment you manipulate responses, you treat people as machines. And manipulating people like rats or machines at times characterizes our evangelism as well.

I do not accuse my fellow Christians of holding the view that man is a mere machine. I know only too well that they, theoretically at least, subscribe to the beliefs that man *is* a soul, that he *has* a spirit and that he is responsible for his actions. This is why evangelism opens a more serious question about the way Christians view their fellow men and women. It is one thing to treat them as laboratory rats in order to open their billfolds. It becomes altogether a more serious matter when we do so to psych them into the kingdom.

Does God sweep people into his kingdom by by-passing their minds and wills? To read some descriptions of revivals would lead us to think so. Yet Scripture teaches otherwise. "We have renounced disgraceful, underhanded ways; we refuse to practice cunning or to tamper with God's word, but by the open statement of the truth we would commend ourselves to every man's conscience in the sight of God" (2 Cor. 4:2).

It seems that Scripture consistently reflects the approach that I address myself *first* to people's understanding ("by the open statement of the truth") and *second* to their consciences ("we would commend ourselves to every man's conscience in the sight of God"). If I am faithful in doing this I may discover that people's *emotions* are also affected and that their *volition* responds with decision and faith. But the order is supremely important: understanding, conscience, emotion, will. I must not appeal directly to emotions but to the mind.

Thus the revival described in Nehemiah 8 began with a reading and explanation of the Scriptures "so that the people understood the reading" (Neh. 8:8). When they understood their error, their consciences were pricked and their emotions aroused.

Unfortunately you can stir people's emotions without their understanding being enlightened at all. But only that stirring which springs from an enlightened understanding and a quickened conscience does justice to our true nature. Anything less insults us and dishonors God.

For many years I have felt something was profoundly wrong with modern evangelism. So deep was my concern that at one stage in my life I was swept perilously toward permanent agnosticism. The uncanny resemblance between evangelistic campaigns and sales campaigns undermined my confidence in what the evangelists said. Only as I gained an understanding of the self-revelation of God in history and of the historicity of Christ's resurrection from the dead did I also gain a deep and quiet assurance that even modern evangelism could not shake.

I became a Christian as a child of eight. Ironically my conversion took place in a large marquee where an Irish evangelist preached an old-fashioned gospel. My two most vivid impressions are the smell of fresh wood shavings and the phrase "substitutionary atonement." I requested of my mother a definition of the latter, and when it was given, I remember saying without any hesitation, "Well, then, I'm saved." No one told me to "witness"; indeed, I would not have understood what the word meant. Yet the day following my conversion I found myself telling my bewildered friends at school what had happened to me.

As the years passed I attended many gospel services and

campaigns. At first all went well. But the older I grew and the more I heard and saw of the preaching of the gospel, the more deeply my faith was shaken. Any "worldly influences" I might have been subject to played little if any part in making me doubt. I grew well acquainted with Scripture, and in the religious instruction classes at school I frequently stood up alone and openly opposed the instructor's attacks on Scripture. So vehement was my opposition that I was asked to attend no more classes in religion but to spend the period in the school library. I did so, defiantly memorizing long passages of the New Testament.

The opponents of Christianity have never caused me to doubt. Only the preachers of the gospel sowed doubts in my heart by creating what nowadays might be called a credibility gap. I had a fondness for literature and read voraciously both modern and romantic novels and poetry. Instinctively I began to see the relationship between truth and great literature. I could not at that stage have expressed the matter in words, but as in my mind I compared the evangelists I knew with Dickens, with Shakespeare, with Tolstoy and with Dostoyevsky, I felt instinctively that good writers were more honest than good evangelists. The comparison increased the credibility gap in my mind.

My disturbance grew deeper as I began to take an active part in evangelistic campaigns. In the course of time I started to act as a counselor and to encounter the kind of people who "went forward" and "made a profession" but woke up the next morning wondering what hit them. No amount of discussion with some of these persons served to convince them of the truth of Scripture or the reality of what had happened to them in the evangelistic meeting. In fact the experience embittered them, leaving them with a deep hostility to the gospel that seemed impossible to quell.

Brainwashed Converts   One night when I watched a TV interview of an American businessman who had been brainwashed into signing false confessions in Hungary, I saw where the problem lay. For the first time I began to suspect that what appeared to be Christian conversions might often be nothing more than brainwashing.

The thought that conversion may at times have no spiritual dimension but be exclusively psychological may seem shocking. Nevertheless it is a fact.

Conversion, of course *is* a psychological phenomenon. *Psychological* means "pertaining to the mind"; *phenomenon* means "something that can be observed." All conversions involve a change of mind and a change that becomes evident to others (and can therefore be observed). What distinguishes Christian conversion from all other types of conversion is that the former is accompanied by regeneration or new birth. Christian conversion occurs when the change in attitude is associated with a sowing of the living Word in the mind of the believer and the springing forth of a new life from God.

In some parts of the world (notably in China) Western evangelistic techniques have been used to convert students to communism. Large student meetings were held in China following the revolution. Enthusiastic communist "evangelists" harangued the crowds with the gospel according to Mao. Young communist converts gave popcorn testimonies. Songs were taught and sung. Emotional appeals were conducted, and ardent personal workers dealt with inquirers. As students yielded themselves to the new faith the light of joy would break over their faces, and a new sense of purpose and commitment characterized their lives.

What happens in the emotional life of someone who is converted (in a Christian or in any other sense)? We still have a lot to learn, but it would seem that prior to many conversion experiences people grow increasingly anxious and tense, and may feel profoundly guilty. At a point where the distress reaches a peak, they suddenly experience a radical change in their orientation to life and goals. At the same time they are suffused with relief and a profound sense of peace and joy. My purpose here is not to discuss technical psychological laws but to point to dangers of which most Christians are unaware and to show how the commercialization of Christian activity has been partly to blame.

Anyone who knows how can produce conversions. They need not be true Christian conversions, but they will be real in the sense that the person undergoing the experience will experience revolutionary changes in his feelings and outlook. For anyone so heartless as to try the experiment, the rules are as follows:

1. *Make people anxious.* You can do this in a number of ways. One way is to make frequent changes in the noise levels of the room. It is now well established that changes in perceptual input create anxiety. If you are speaking, try yelling at the top of your lungs, then dropping your voice to a menacing whisper. It doesn't matter too much what you say at this point so long as you use your voice properly. Use singing and musical instruments in the same way. Amplifiers can help greatly. The important thing is to work up to a crescendo, then let the sound sink into a velvety silence punctuated by soft but clearly enunciated syllables such as, "And ... this ... my friend ... is ... what ... may happen ... to you." Let the silence go on for a few seconds, then

begin immediately yelling at a decibel level slightly higher than your previous crescendo. Many of the people listening to you will find their underarm deodorants have stopped working, that their mouths are dry and that their pulses have quickened.

2. *Induce guilt.* Most people spend a lot of mental energy keeping guilty thoughts at bay. So inducing guilt is not difficult once you discuss a few sins with the volume modulations that I described in Rule 1. Speak as one who knows. Or better still, tell your audience that God knows about the dirty little thing that is festering in the minds of so many present. Once you've got them anxious, it is fairly easy to make them guilty. Repetition is valuable at this point.

3. *Destroy their judgment.* This is more difficult. The best way is to switch frequently the *emotional tone* of the meeting. If you are good at weepy stories, tell one as skillfully as you can. Then grow solemn and try the up-and-down volume technique. Make like you're angry and indignant. Talk about the awful calamities that are coming on society: war, earthquakes, pollution. Then instead of doing the velvety silence sequence tell them a joke. You'll be amazed at the response. It has nothing to do with your skill as a comedian. It is only an index of the anxiety present. They are laughing from relief at this point. After this go back to something weepy. Before long your experimental rats will have lost touch with all the normal bearings by which they know what is what, and you will find that many of them are putty in your hands.

4. *Repeat the same cliché over and over again.* It doesn't really matter whether they understand what you're saying or not. At this point you are communicating on a nonverbal level anyway. It's more the rhythm and the emotional tone that's

getting through than the content. Some Christian evangelists find it very effective at this point to get the choir to sing very softly. Any faint moans from the converted will help create the mood you're striving for. And whether it's money you're after, dedications or professions of conversion, all you have to do is pull in the net.

5. *For camps and conferences you should encourage exhaustion.* Communists have found this effective when dealing with prisoners. Emotional and physical exhaustion, especially when it is associated with lack of sleep, helps to weaken any resistance to the brainwashing process.

Am I being heartlessly cynical? Am I perhaps making a mockery of the Holy Spirit's power? Not at all. I am exposing some contemporary practices. For in our spiritual harlotry we are conceiving children, but too often they are bastards who will never inherit glory.

The kind of thing that I have been talking about exists not only in the dramatic way I have described. When someone is converted to communism, a profound change occurs affecting the person's whole life. But the change may be gradual. What matters is that it be brought about.

The decision again might only be a trivial one. In countless ways I am subject all day long to influences which fashion my actions. Images of sight or sound from innumerable sources wash my brain to influence me to purchase this or that, to vote for one candidate or another, or to give money to this or that cause. Vance Packard has dealt with the processes in detail in his book *The Hidden Persuaders.* The underlying philosophy of the techniques is materialist. Only a machine can be made to do what we want by pressing the right buttons or pulling the right levers. It is therefore assumed consciously or unconsciously either that man is such a machine or that the machinelike part of him is the part that matters.

That non-Christian capitalists or communist totalitarian states should so manipulate people to promote their interests surprises me little. But that Christian organizations, proud of their belief that people are free moral agents made in the image of God, should treat them like laboratory rats appalls me. I can only wonder at such a dichotomy between our professed beliefs and our overt actions.

You may ask me, "Is there no place for emotion in preaching?" Obviously there is. I do not protest against emotion but against its artificial manipulation. Sometimes when I preach I find it hard to suppress my tears. The preacher who understands the solemnity of his message has something to weep about. But I would sooner have a weeping preacher and a dry-eyed congregation than a skillful preacher who is himself unmoved, save by a joy in his capacity to make the congregation weep.

My atheist acquaintances may smile at this point and suggest to me that manipulation pays off. When we treat people like machines, they respond like machines; therefore, they must *be* machines.

In this book there is hardly room to do justice to the point. It is true that our central nervous system has many of the qualities of a computer. It is also true that many of our *actions* seem computer controlled. When you sit on a pin, you jump. No rational decision, carefully weighed and considered, precedes your leap from pain. The action is mechanical. And so is the anger you automatically feel when your bloodstream is flushed with adrenalin.

If you had to figure out what to do every time you sat on a pin, your conscious life would be cluttered with trivia. In fact some forms of mental illness consist of precisely such a cluttering. I see patients sometimes who are so obsessed with whether they should carry a handkerchief in their left-hand trouser pocket or their right-hand trouser pocket, and whether the handkerchief should be changed five times a day or six times a day that they are no longer free to live, to love and to enjoy the glory of life.

Human beings are, of course, made in the image of God. This is what gives each of us our infinite value. To treat people like things, like machines (even if they respond like machines) is sin. It is contrary to God's entire purpose for the world which seeks to lift each of us to the full glory he originally planned.

A Bearer of News   Therefore I call not in my own name, but in the name of the sovereign Christ of God, upon anyone who presumes to regard himself as a preacher of the gospel to have done with preacher's tricks. I don't care how wide your radio or TV coverage is or whether you preach in a tiny frame building in the boondocks. Your first job as a preacher is to *inform*. You are a bearer of news. It is news that must be explained clearly and in detail. There need be no journalistic tricks to play on sensational angles. Let us have done with tabloid preaching. Let us also have done with pandering to popular fads and fashions. (Once it was communism. Then it became the joys of sanctified sex techniques.) The good news is that God became man, lived, taught, died and rose. He is now glorified and will come to judge the world in righteousness.

The Holy Spirit can only touch people's consciences if their minds have been enlightened with clearly enunciated good news. "We refuse to practice cunning or to tamper with God's word, but by the open statement of the truth we would commend ourselves to every man's conscience in the sight of God" (2 Cor. 4:2). Truth is for the mind not the emotions. Your first job is to inform the *minds* of men and women with *facts.* If you do that the Holy Spirit will awaken their consciences. Only when people's consciences are awakened by the Holy Spirit can their emotions properly be stirred. And even then God will only stir them by awakening them to the true gravity of their condition and the wonder of Christ's love. Such awakening, such stirring is God's part, not yours. Your job is to *inform* not to dabble with wills and emotions.

And the same applies to you who are not preachers. Your job, likewise, is to inform your colleagues of plain facts. To explain them. To show their relevance. Christ is not a product to be marketed, nor are those to whom you witness customers.

Origin, Identity, Owner   Much earlier in this book I stated that the essence of harlotry was to forget who we are, from whence we came and to whom we belong. Perhaps we should look at the definition more closely as we re-evaluate our approach to evangelism.

From Whence We Came. When I look at a colleague at work, hardened in his sin and unbelief, it sometimes seems impossible for me to see how he could possibly become a Christian. So wide is the gap between our thinking, so self-assured and at ease does my friend seem that my prayers die on my lips. Even God could not arouse such from darkness.

I am walking, of course, by sight rather than by faith at this point. I am believing in the visible more than in the invisible Holy Spirit. Nevertheless my dilemma is a real one. A hopelessness has descended on my soul that seems impossible to shake off. Unless. . . .

Unless I could somehow get him to a meeting where. . . .

Unless I could somehow get him to read. . . .

Unless I could introduce him to. . . .

What is wrong with my reasoning? It is wrong simply because it reveals that I can only believe an invisible God will work *if I can see some visible means by which he will do so.* I can believe if my friend will come to the meeting. If not I really don't see how. And this is the point at which idolatry begins. You may say, "But it's not in the *preacher* I'm believing but in the God behind the preacher!" And that is exactly what idol worshipers say. "It is not in the piece of stone we believe, but in the god behind it."

Don't get me wrong. I too preach and write and meet people. But you would be turning me into an idol if you believed God would save your friend only through my instrumentality or through some similar visible, understandable device. So long as seeing is believing, believing is still unbelief.

Were you a likely candidate for salvation? Yet didn't God save you? And while he may have used some human instrument, don't you see that he would have saved you with or without any instrument? And haven't you seen other "impossible" brothers and sisters delivered likewise by the incredible power of the invisible God?

Do you realize from whence you came? You were in the grip of hell. Demons had wrapped their chains about you. The god of this world had blinded your understanding. Yet God struck off your chains and the face of Christ illumined your soul. The damned around you are no more damned than you were, their chains no thicker, their darkness no deeper. Nor is the power of Christ to save them one whit less.

Our modern evangelistic methods display our tragic unbelief in the power of God because we have already forgotten the pit from which all of us alike were dragged by divine power. Therefore we have to rely on methods that work, that is, whose working we can see.

Who We Are. We are children of God, not children of science. Science can only explore the fringes of God's laws. We are not in the business of pseudospiritual brainwashing. We do not belong among experimental psychologists or the pathetic ranks of sales armies.

We are the followers of the Lamb. We tread in the footsteps of apostles and martyrs. We do not gauge the success of our preaching by the number of our converts but by its clear adherence to the truth. We are those who are to be filled with the Holy Spirit. We would rather be laughed to scorn and thrown to the lions than descend to gimmicks and trickery to turn on a crowd at an evangelistic meeting.

We are clothed in garments of salvation. Angels and demons look on to see what we will do. We bear the mark of God upon our foreheads. We are citizens of heaven, future judges of the universe, fellow heirs with Christ. Let us beware lest we forget the high dignity of our calling.

To Whom We Belong. We belong in practice to whomever or whatever we display our allegiance. We owe our allegiance to Christ. None of us would deny it. But the essence of harlotry lies in looking to other sources for what our true bridegroom gives us freely.

And what will he not give? Does he not now sit at the right hand of God? Has he not told us that all authority in heaven and earth lies between his fingers? Is he not the author whose writing creates the history enacted before our eyes? Has he not sent his Spirit? Is the Spirit not even this moment working in the minds and hearts of millions who as yet have heard no word of Christian testimony? Did he or did he not rise from the tomb? Did he or did he not make the sun stand still, open the waters of the Red Sea, cause the walls of Jericho to fall with a trumpet blast? Has he not for twenty centuries created revivals, reformations and awakenings without any mechanical aid that we could devise?

And do we or do we not belong to him? The question is a solemn one, for in my ears I hear querulous voices of the future pleading, "Lord did we not organize rallies in your name and in your name bring thousands to the Exhibition Hall? Lord did we not put on a television show that brought in thousands of dollars for your cause?" And for some of these the answer will be, "Depart from me you workers of iniquity into outer darkness. For I never knew you."

10

SORROW, STORMS AND SUNRISE

"Plead with your mother, plead . . ." (Hos. 2:2).

More than once I have walked with a forsaken husband round his deserted house. Each time, by coincidence, night has made darkness darker and emptiness more hollow. Each time the man's voice was flat, incredulous, bewildered. "It's funny. You know, I can't believe it's happened." Then, pensively, "The children's beds are all gone. She must have had it organized somehow." Or "She's left my books and records, and taken her own." Or "She's taken all the kids' pictures." Some litter usually lay around. A forgotten toy would be in a corner. We would mechanically empty the garbage and check on the contents of the refrigerator. I remember sitting down on an old settee with one man. "What shall I do, John? What shall I do?"

Perhaps from the bitterness of her heart a wife could

have given a fitting reply. I am not trying to take up cudgels on behalf of deserted husbands. Wives, too, are deserted every day to experience similar shock and pain. It is to pain I point.

"Plead with your mother, *plead*. . . ." As numbness wears off, an agony of longing makes itself felt. "I would do anything, *anything*. . . . I can see I've been at fault, made many mistakes. But this seems so final."

Hosea may or may not have made mistakes. We are not told. But God, whose voice we are now listening to, made none. "Plead, *plead*." God pleading? God feeling pain?

Whenever I have been involved with a deserted husband or wife I have noticed something else. Once the decision is made, the deserter (man or woman) finds ways to cut himself or herself off from being exposed to the pain of the person deserted. Distance. No address. A sudden, well-planned departure with a curt, cold note about communication via a lawyer. Unlisted phone numbers. At all costs and by all means the deserter must be shielded from the sights and sounds of wounds he or she has inflicted.

In fact the preparation to ward off pain has sometimes been taking place for months. Psychological as well as physical barriers have been constructed. "I don't feel anything for him now." "I just don't love her anymore." "There's nothing there. It's all over between us."

So the deserted party is doubly cut off, logistically and psychologically. Into a blank wall a heart cries with inarticulate pleading, echoed but unheard.

Two things puzzle us about God's grief over his people. In the first place we find it hard to believe that God should be upset about our materialism. We are also puzzled

that God should feel the pain of desertion. He is self-suffi-
cient, infinite. He has no needs. He pours out riches
without lessening anything of what he has or is. There is
nothing we can contribute which will add a jot to him. Yet
he pleads, feels pain, cries out with longing. Cries to a
church that has shielded herself from his pain, a church
that refuses to look into his weeping eyes or that feels a
strange emptiness where love once burned. If there is a
wonder greater than God reduced to a helpless infant in a
barn, it is the wonder of an infinite God torn with an agony
of longing for a people who have forsaken him and that
have no awareness of his pain.

Of course these wonders are one. The cry, "Plead,
plead"; the kicking, diapered infant; the tortured form,
wracked in darkness on a gibbet: all three are one. In all
three we see the marvel of God's pain because of a harlot.

It is pain for the harlot's fate not pain for himself. Pain
lest he do what he must do, "lest I strip her naked . . . and
slay her with thirst" (Hos. 2:3). "Therefore I will take back
my grain in its time, and my wine in its season; and I will
take away my wool and my flax, which were to cover her
nakedness. Now I will uncover her lewdness in the sight of
all her lovers, and no one shall rescue her out of my hand"
(Hos. 2:9-10).

Our problem with a punitive God is that we are ourselves
bitter and vindictive. "It hurts me more than it hurts you,"
has a hollow ring from human lips. God's agony on the
other hand is free of venom. It is agony beyond anything we
can understand, but agony he feels on our behalf. He
knows, because he is holy, what he must do. Holiness and
love clash fiercely so that fires rage in his bosom, selfless
fires in a God of holiness and love. He takes no pleasure in

stripping, in starving, in exposing. He has no joy in the death of the wicked, only an infinite pain.

Yet he will do what he must. His attitude to sin is inflexible. He will not stay his hand however long he may delay it. He will warn, threaten, plead. But finally he will act, and when he does his judgments will be as thorough as they are unswerving. It has been so throughout the Scripture, throughout church history, and it will remain so till the end of time.

So when he pleads with the Western church, he does so because of what he can see lying ahead of us, not only for those of us who are leaders and therefore more responsible, but for those who are our children and have followed us. "Upon her children also I will have no pity" (Hos. 2:4).

Children don't always realize what is happening to start with. Even when they do and cry, "Where is mommy? I want mommy!" they soon learn to suppress the longings of their little hearts. They learn that in some obscure sense the missing parent is now the enemy. If you want to keep the affection of the parent you still have, you learn (even if you are only four or five years old) to be relatively discreet about your feelings toward the enemy.

So it is the children (as we are reminded time without number) who suffer. And historically it has always seemed that the judgments of God appear to fall indiscriminately upon villains and their offspring. When foreign armies overran Israel or Judah, the heads of little ones would be dashed against the rocks, the women raped, the aged tossed over a precipice.

We are sickened by the horror of it all and avoid those pages of Scripture which implicate God's judgments in such atrocities. We prefer to worship a different god, made up of our favorite selections from Scripture. Many Bible scholars have grappled with moral problems of God's divine judgment through the historical process, and I will not add here to what they have said except to say that there are things more important than physical survival.

Hosea's only comment concerns *why* God's judgment falls on children of harlotry. It is because they are just that, children of harlotry. Just as David's first child with Bathsheba died, so will many of our own. And if we pause to think for a moment we may see that should God's judgment fall upon the twentieth-century church, it must inevitably fall on many who have been conceived in idolatry and fed on the milk of materialistic unbelief. Like mother, like daughter; like father, like son. We have reared a brood of children who are ours but who may not, whatever they profess with their lips, be children of God at all. Evangelical churches, fundamentalist churches, liberal Protestant and Catholic churches are full of people who have gone through some form of Christianization (be it baptism or going forward) but whom we have taught to trust in dollars and in technology more than in the ascended Christ.

Judgment and Persecution And what form will his judgment take?

The New Testament teaches, this we have already seen, that the Lord of the church judges both churches and evildoers. You can say what you like Whether you insist that Revelation 2—3 is addressed to real first-century churches or that here Jesus addresses future church ages, it is all one. Christ pronounces judgment on his people.

In the book of Revelation he makes several different threats. "I will come to you and remove your lampstand from its place, unless you repent" (2:5). "I will come to you soon and war against them with the sword of my mouth" (2:16). "I will throw her on a sickbed, and those who commit adultery with her I will throw into great tribulation, unless they repent of her doings; and I will strike her children dead" (2:22-23). "I will spew you out of my mouth" (3:16).

We could say the judgments were of two sorts—spiritual and physical. "I will remove your lampstand." (I will remove my holy presence from your midst. You will have no power, no warmth, no true light, no life. You will become a dead, empty shell of a church, a building where people congregate, a purely human activity bereft of any touch of heaven.) "I will war against them with the sword of my mouth." (God's Word will cut down the unrepentant with shattering power. The hammer will break the rock in pieces.) While the imagery John uses is physical, the judgments described here are spiritual. One of them is negative (the removal of spiritual presence); the other is positive (the terrifying power of the convicting Word). But physical judgments are spoken of too—sickness, tribulation, death.

How are we to understand them? We can conceive physical judgments on the nation of Israel. Foreign armies overran her, raped her, took her people into captivity. But how can we conceive of foreign armies in relation to the church? And if physical persecution falls on the church, how may we distinguish between divine judgment and Satanic opposition? When communist-inspired rioters burn down a church building or when secret police seize Christian leaders in the cold hours before dawn, how do we interpret what is happening?

Clearly both kinds of trouble await us. There will be divine judgments executed against a harlot church unless she repents, and they may sometimes take a physical form. There will also be Satan-inspired persecution against the faithful. Infidelity will be rewarded with judgment, faithfulness with persecution. We may make our grim choice. But if we are to talk of judgment, we must remember something else. Judgment is ongoing as well as ultimate. It proceeds throughout history as well as in one final wind-up. We must also remember that God judges sin in nations as well as in churches, and while he clearly will differentiate in his expectations and in his reaction to each, the means by which judgment will descend on both need not differ.

If we take what has happened under right-wing and left-wing tyranny during the present century, we may begin to see how it all works out in practice. Tyranny overcomes a people. At times both people and church are affected, though perhaps in different ways. Churches may be asked by tyrannical governments (for example, in China, in Cuba, in Nazi Germany, in right-wing Chile) to collaborate with the government in maintaining order. The appeal seems innocent enough, even scriptural. It involves organizations or religious bodies in such a way that an authority structure can extend from government to the local congregation.

But slowly its evils become apparent. A church may be expected to extol a political leader. I remember the tears and sighs of a Christian student years ago who described church life under Trujillo in what is now the Dominican Republic. "My father was an elder in our assembly and a member of the secret police," he told me. "His spiritual life was virtually nil. His influence in the church was exercised mainly through me. On Trujillo Day I was expected to speak at several churches on the virtues of Trujillo. I knew what the secret police were doing. Some of my friends had been tortured. Yet if I refused to preach the praises of Trujillo, not only was my dad in trouble, but there would be reprisals against the church. My mother would come and weep before me until I consented to do it."

It is a common story, and I could multiply examples of the subtle and complex situations arising. They are not few. Nero worship was a problem facing the church in the first century.

What happens under such an oppressive regime is that the church slowly moves into a position of compromise over spiritual issues (that is to say, over who is Lord, Jesus or the current head of state). If it fails to do so it is obliged to accept all the consequences of being secretly "uncooperative." The church that compromises, that accepts alliance in the state is stripped like the harlot she is and shamed. She is stripped of all real authority. The government smiles scornfully at her leaders. The head of the secret police has them all in his pocket. Everyone, people and government alike, know what the real score is. She is stripped of honor, stripped of pride, stripped of glory, stripped sometimes of property and assigned inferior places to meet in. Her autonomy is gone. She is the slave and tool of the state.

It would seem that the most terrible judgments of God toward the church are not physical but spiritual. The candlestick is removed. The harlot is made bare. She is exposed in her shame for all to see.

God's physical judgments seem on the other hand to be exercised against individuals or parties *within* a living church and are designed to cut out a cancer, leaving the church bleeding but ready to be healed. There should be no problem in distinguishing between Satanic opposition and divine judgment. What we may underestimate is the shame, depression and empty futility of the life of the church that has become a collaborator of the modern state.

We are in fact already making ourselves vulnerable to such a fate. Not only have we accepted Western values, becoming worshipers of the golden cow, turning ourselves from churches into Christian business enterprises, Christian industries and Christian social clubs, but we have made it clear that to be a good Christian is to be a good American, a good Canadian, a good Briton or whatever. The distinction between citizenship of heaven and earthly citizenship is becoming blurred. Jeremiah, whose loyalty to Judah never faltered (for he never ceased to serve Judah's true interests) wound up being regarded as a traitor to his country. Few modern Christians are in any such danger. We accept all too naively the essential rightness of the country we live in. And pain, terrible pain awaits us. Years of aching and longing. Years of emptiness and meaninglessness. Happy are they who are tortured and go to jail, for they shall know the glory of the Lord! Woe to those who bow to Nero, for they shall hunger and lack bread; they shall thirst and have no drink, shiver and remain naked to winds of the North.

Values Changed by Adversity But our God is a God of mercy. Even his punishments have restoration in mind. "Therefore I will hedge up her way with thorns; and I will build a wall against her, so that she cannot find her paths. She shall pursue her lovers, . . . but shall not find them. Then shall she say, 'I will go and return to my first husband, for it was better with me then than now' " (Hos. 2:6-7).

It is curious how pain, adversity and danger can change our values. I met a man who was trapped for hours in the cabin of an overturned semitrailer. Gasoline had dripped over him as he lay there helplessly. Cold and snow reduced his chances of rescue. And even when he was found, there was the drawn-out problem of getting him free.

How many thoughts raced through his mind! Things that had seemed of paramount importance hours before suddenly became of no account. The foolish urge to deliver his goods on time. Personal relationships. Time itself and how to use it. What life was for. What he would do with twenty-four hours of freedom if he could have them.

When eventually he stood on his feet, free, uninjured, staring at the half-buried wreckage, he was staring at a life that no longer existed. It lay with the ruins of the semitrailer. He was a changed man, seeing things as he had never seen them before. And his new vision corresponded with truer values than his old one. Pain and danger had led him to truth.

Chuck Colson tells in his book *Born Again* how the pressures of Watergate and even the dehumanization of prison totally changed his perspective on life and was used by God to draw him into a tender love relationship with him. The same story could be repeated with a thousand variations. It is not that adversity merely changes our behavior. It changes the way we see things. And our new vision can be a doorway to joy, to peace, to unimaginable liberty. There are signs of repentance and longing in some compromising churches under communist oppression.

The devil, of course, has his deadly counterfeit of the same process by which pain changes our view of life. A political prisoner is thrown in jail. He cannot sleep in his cell for the lights glare, and he is awakened at irregular intervals. At times he is dragged and roughly thrust into the presence of accusing officials who bully him with threats, frighten him with a surprising knowledge of his past life, dismay him by showing him a letter from his wife (perhaps a forged one) telling him she has left him for someone else. He may be subject to torture or beatings and be left half-starved with no medical attention.

But then, unexpectedly comes kindness—the mild, understanding official, offering a cigarette, solicitous about all the prisoner has been through, showing him he is a tragic victim of a heartless capitalistic imperialism. The prisoner, too, begins to see things differently. The world he once believed in grows strangely unreal, distorted. A new set of ideas suddenly seems obvious, real. Why has he never understood before? It all seems so clear, now.

Is God a washer of brains?

There are profound differences between the God of the prophets and political brainwashers. God has no interest in manipulating results. He could if he so desired change our life view by a snap of his fingers. He would have no need to resort to a play on our feelings. By a simple word he could make us insane so that we would say black was white and red was green. He does not need techniques and equipment. He is not a manipulator. He proved that when he gave us the power to choose.

Moreover his tenderness is not fake. It is not an act designed to play on our weakness but the revelation of his very heart. And when we will let him, he does not turn us over to an underling but condescends to draw near himself. Finally he is interested in truth. He is truth. His only object is to help see the truth. Seeing the truth, we can make a meaningful choice. Acting on truth will make us free.

"Therefore, behold, I will allure her ... and speak tenderly to her" (Hos. 2:14). The picture is a beautiful one. To woo is not to seduce. The seducer plays on feelings to gain a selfish end; the lover woos to overcome those fears that prevent a lost woman from becoming a princess. The seducer manipulates; the wooer shows genuine kindness and understanding. The seducer yearns to get; the wooer, to give.

Yet in each case the process is a delicate one. It must be gentle for it is resisted by fear and mistrust. And the fear is understandable. God is a God of fiery rage. What we do not see is that his rage concerns our sin. His tenderness concerns ourselves. But because we are human we are nervous about this untamed God of fire. We are wild birds needing to learn trust. We neither see what is there nor hear what is said. If we are Beauty, we can see only the Beast. We may have heard his stern denunciations, but we have never learned to hear the music of a love that passes knowledge.

Is it not a marvel that God should take time to woo? "Take it or leave it," says the rich film star who offers a wedding ring to a starlet. And if she takes the ring, she finds she has to take it off a year later. Yet here comes one who loves us with an everlasting love and who is in no hurry. He takes time. He speaks gently. If his wooing becomes urgent, it never ceases to be tender. But it may not be until we have suffered that our eyes are open to see, our ears to hear, our hearts to feel.

The Door of Restoration "I will ... make the Valley of Achor a door of hope" (Hos. 2:15). I cannot, I suppose, address the church as a whole, but only you who read. The Valley of Achor was a valley where terrible judgment fell on Achan and his family (Josh. 7:20-26). We shudder to read of a wholesale burning and stoning, and the pile of rocks heaped over the charred bones of those on whom God's judgment fell. We wonder how fair it was that Achan's family should have suffered as well. But we must be realists rather than moralists. Our actions do affect others. A father's unwise speculations reduce his family to poverty, or his alcoholism may subject them to violence, hunger and fear. Not that God would have it so. He deplores the fact that children suffer for their parents' sins (Ezek. 18). However, you yourself may be facing even now, not only the personal pain of the Lord's discipline, but the unspoken agony of being responsible that his judgments affect those most dear to you.

The Valley of Achor is intended to be a door of hope. God's object is to restore his relationship with you. Until that relationship is restored you cannot heal the pain of others. Only one who is healed can heal. And God waits to draw near to you. He waits to turn dryness into streams of water and flower-filled meadows, to turn loneliness into fellowship, purposelessness into purpose, emptiness into fullness of joy. The very catastrophe that may have fallen on you is itself your greatest opportunity if only you will see it.

Review your position. Review your priorities. What have you been insisting on so fiercely? What is the something you have vowed never to give way on? Are you so sure you are right in the stand you have taken? You *may* be, but is God trying to shed new light on your circumstances? Take time to weigh matters again. Do not be afraid of what you may have to let go. Expose yourself, if you have to, to the humiliation of being in the wrong. So you have been a fool or worse. So people will smile and say, "I always said he was wrong!" You are not the first. The door of hope in the Valley of Achor may have a low lintel. Bow your head a little as you step through. The new world into which you will pass will soon dissolve your humiliations in a deeper joy than you have yet known. A. W. Tozer wrote in his book *The Pursuit of God,*

> Before the Lord God made man upon the earth He first prepared for him by creating a world of useful and pleasant things for his sustenance and delight. In the Genesis account of the creation these are called simply "things." They were made for man's uses, but they were meant always to be external to the man and subservient to him. In the deep heart of the man was a shrine where none but God was worthy to come. Within him was God; without, a thousand gifts which God had showered upon him.
>
> But sin has introduced complications and has made those very gifts of God a potential source of ruin to the soul.
>
> Our woes began when God was forced out of His central shrine and "things" were allowed to enter. Within the human heart "things" have taken over. Men have now by nature no peace within their hearts, for God is crowned there no longer, but there in the moral dusk stubborn and aggressive usurpers fight among themselves for first place on the throne.

How do we rid ourselves of those "stubborn and aggressive usurpers" that fight in the moral dusk "among themselves for first place on the throne"?

I remember a night some years ago pacing the length of a beautiful tropical beach and crying out to God to be delivered from the power of mammon forever. God has answered and is still answering my prayer. Things still attract me, but I now know what I really want. Tozer also wrote,

The man who has God for his treasure has all things in One. Many ordinary treasures may be denied him, or if he is allowed to have them, the enjoyment of them will be so tempered that they will never be necessary to his happiness. Or if he must see them go, one after one, he will scarcely feel a sense of loss, for having the Source of all things he has in One all satisfaction, all pleasure, all delight. Whatever he may lose he has actually lost nothing, for he now has it all in One, and he has it purely, legitimately and forever.

A choice faces you. There is not room for two treasures in your heart. Which would you choose if you had to, God or things? The question is vital and must be answered now, before the day of testing comes on you.

The Future of the Church   But you may be wondering about the church we both love. What of her future? What will happen when freedom falls down about our ears here in the West (as it surely will sooner or later)? How will the church survive?

Certainly she will not survive in her present outward form. Certainly her whoredoms will be painfully, humiliatingly exposed. Undoubtedly some groups will suffer both unthinkable persecutions and unspeakable glories. God has not changed, nor has the nature of evil. History is still in some measure repeating itself. The twentieth century need not expect to escape all that has been going on for centuries. It seems rather to be bringing the strands of world history together.

Dark clouds fill the horizon. Perhaps every century has had a sense of the apocalyptic, but the twentieth has more reason to have it than most. We are a global village. We are no longer a vast world but a shrunken spaceship, our lives bound together inexorably by an invisible network of communications. The twentieth century *is* unique. Humankind can for the first time destroy itself. Our technological powers have reached their zenith while our moral capacity remains as feeble as ever. Our knowledge has never been greater, our wisdom never more abysmal.

You may ask me, "Are you saying that the church will pass through the Great Tribulation?" I counter, what does it matter? In two-thirds of the world the church is already passing through great tribulation, and she will pass, come what may, through the same here in the West. The point is not will the tribulation be the Tribulation or the great be Great, but will it be or not be? I tell you that unless deep and widespread repentance comes, terrible tribulation will take place in the West.

The night will grow darker. If we are appalled at all that is happening around us, we have only begun to see the unleashed furies of blackness. The final Dark Ages are beginning. Mankind shall dwell for many days without sun to light its gloom or shelter from the furies of the storm. And the church, like Hosea's bride will suffer with it. Yet, as in the words of Gerhard Tersteegen's hymn,

Midst the darkness, storm, and sorrow,
  One bright gleam I see;
Well I know the blessed morrow
  Christ will come for me. . . .
He and I, in that bright glory,
  One deep joy shall share—
Mine, to be for ever with Him;
  His, that I am there.

While God's judgments upon humankind serve the interests of justice, his judgments on his people serve those of mercy.

"And in that day, says the LORD, you will call me, 'My husband,' and no longer will you call me, '[My golden cow].' For I will remove the names of the [false gods] from her mouth, and they shall be mentioned by name no more.... And I will betroth you to me for ever; I will betroth you to me in righteousness and in justice, in steadfast love, and in mercy. I will betroth you to me in faithfulness; and you shall know the LORD" (Hos. 2:16-17, 19-20).

In the meantime we need not preoccupy ourselves with the details of the program. During World War 2 when bombs rained ruin from the skies on Britain, some self-styled experts argued fiercely about the precise manner in which the war would end, endlessly debating the fate of the Italians, the role of the Americans in Italy, in France, scheduling and rescheduling the order of events. These Britons argued inside bomb shelters while London burned.

Other Britons wore helmets to protect their heads from the hot jagged shrapnel that fell like hailstones, dug among the rubble of ruined homes and factories, dragged men and women from burning ruins, drove ambulances. Yet others looked through gunsights around the city or flew tiny fighter planes below the stars, also peering through gunsights.

Some talked. Some fought. Doubtless the experts felt in some obscure way that the war was in their hands. Psychologically they needed to feel in control and their talk, their pseudoexpertise, gave them the security that bomb shelters alone could not provide. Meanwhile the real war was going on where shrapnel fell and bombs exploded.

It is so today. We are called on to fight, not to be experts on the end times. We are called to bear witness in life or death to the King of glory.

Let me shift my metaphor. The church is not called to be attractive in the end times. She is not to paint herself and play the role of hussy. Whenever she has been faithful throughout history she has been mocked, vilified, scorned. If she is faithful now, the same fate awaits her. But people will marvel, not at the beauty of a harlot, but at the wonder of a Lord who can hold the faithfulness of his bride in face of so terrible an onslaught. She may be mocked and tortured but her honor will remain unsullied, for she will scorn her persecutors knowing her avenger will not tarry.

He is coming back. He is coming for his bride. He knows that she has failed him often but he is coming to restore her, to reward her, to reveal his glory in her. His enemies will drop their weapons. Proud heads will be bowed. They will see her in a different light because they will see him whom they rejected crowned and glorified.

A Bride and a Painter   I must end on a lighter note. The famous ethologist Konrad Lorenz writes engagingly in *King Solomon's Ring* of the pecking order in his jackdaw colony. He tells the story of Double-aluminium, the new president of the colony, and of Double-aluminium's courtship.

Goldgreen, the old president had conquered the heart of a little, very fragile, and in order of rank, low-standing lady who sidled ever nearer to him to attract his attention. Like the church of today she longed for the smile of the powers that be. But on his arrival Double-aluminium not only took over the leadership of the colony, but wooed and won the "low-standing" lady who had been pursuing Goldgreen.

"Within the course of two days he was publicly engaged to her. Since the partners in a jackdaw marriage support each other loyally and bravely in every conflict, and as no pecking order exists between them, they automatically rank as of equal status in their disputes with all other members of the colony. A wife is therefore, of necessity, raised to her husband's position."

We may look with disapproval upon the fickleness of the lady who so readily switched her affections from one president to another, and we may despise the harlot church for her harlotries, but our eyes should be on our own Double-aluminium. When he comes he will rule. When he comes, his love for his true bride will be greater than the sins of her unfaithfulness. He has loved her with an everlasting love and will bind her to him forever. His foes will suddenly cease to despise her because they will see what she is in relation to him. He will hold her to his side, and her shame will be seen no more.

But his bride, the church, is made of many individuals of whom you are one. You will meet him not only as a member of his body and bride but as his servant, his would-be companion, his soldier, his sheep, his brother, his friend. What is Christ's word to you as the darkness gathers around you and as the conflict thickens?

Are you afraid? "The Lord knows how to rescue the godly from trial" (2 Pet. 2:9). He knows you belong to him. He will not forsake you. He knows how much you can take and senses every longing of your heart. "Fear not," he bids you. "Be strong and of good courage."

Has his coming seemed to tarry? Know then that "with the Lord one day is as a thousand years, and a thousand years as one day. The Lord is not slow about his promise"

(2 Pet. 3:8-9). He will not delay. His coming is indeed at hand. "But the day of the Lord will come like a thief, and then the heavens will pass away with a loud noise, and the elements be dissolved with fire, and the earth and the works that are upon it will be burned up" (2 Pet. 3:10).

What then must you do as catastrophe and judgment loom ahead? "Since all these things are thus to be dissolved, ..." since matter is temporary, honor ephemeral, riches corruptible, real estate highly flammable, human might fragile, mountains mobile, seas made to boil, earth itself to be folded away like a cast-off garment, "since all these things are thus to be dissolved, what sort of persons ought you to be in lives of holiness and godliness, waiting for and hastening [earnestly desiring] the coming of the day of God." For we are to be given "new heavens and a new earth in which righteousness dwells. Therefore ... be zealous to be found by him without spot or blemish, and at peace" (2 Pet. 3:11-14).

Be zealous. Zeal is not a feeling. It is an attitude you adopt. You adopt it deliberately in the face of God's truth. The world will pass away with its lusts. Only he who (because he believes and sees truth for what it is) does the will of God, will abide forever. To be zealous means to act consistently in the light of ultimate reality. We are to be found, if possible, without spot. This means we are to keep short accounts with God. Daily we are to let his Spirit search our hearts. Daily we are to keep our relationship with him a cleansed one that we may walk with him in sweet fellowship now and meet him without shame when he comes.

My friend Peter Forrester was painting a corner of our house the other day from the top of a ladder. The wind blew strongly, and boughs of trees near the corner of the house swayed dizzyingly in the wind. At one point Peter got the strange sensation that the trees were still, and that the house and the ladder were swaying in the wind. He thought to himself, "I know ladders. I know *this* ladder. I know I planted it securely. I know that houses don't sway in the wind but that trees do. Whatever I feel, I *know* what is happening." So he went on painting. He acted on what he knew to be reality.

You are called on to do the same. The reality is not what you see around. Solidity is to be found in a God who rules, a Christ who has redeemed and whose Word will never fail. In the last times you may find yourself painting on the top of the ladder. As the house seems to sway and the trees to stand still, faith will consist of reminding yourself that it is the trees, not the house, that are moving, and zeal will be to go on painting until the job is finished.